With love to Jon,
Greatgrandma and Pona
2020

Dominique Bar, Louis-Bernard Koch, Guy Lehideux

John Paul II

The Journey of a Saint

MAGNIFICAT® • Ignatius

Illustrator: **Dominique Bar.**
Authors: **Louis-Bernard Koch** and **Guy Lehideux.**

Colorist: **Vittorio Leonardo, Marcinelle.**
Some drawings were based on photos by **Arturo Mari** and **Adam Bujak**.

Under the direction of Romain Lizé, Vice President, Magnificat

Translator: Janet Chevrier
Editor, Magnificat: Isabelle Galmiche
Editor, Ignatius: Vivian Dudro
Assistant of the Editor: Pascale Vandewalle
Layout Designers: Élise Borel, Jean-Marc Richard
Proofreader: Cameron Pollette
Production: Thierry Dubus, Sabine Marioni

Original French edition in two volumes:
Volume1: *Avec Jean-Paul II: Karol Wojtyla, de Cracovie a Rome*
© 2008 by Editions du Triomphe, Paris
Volume 2: *Avec Jean-Paul II: L'infatigable pèlerin*
@ 2011 by Editions du Triomphe, Paris

IN 1919, THE TREATY OF VERSAILLES PUTS AN END TO WORLD WAR I. AT LAST, POLAND REGAINS CLEAR BORDERS AND RECLAIMS ITS INDEPENDENCE, LOST IN 1795.

BUT LENIN'S COMMUNIST RUSSIA NOW THREATENS TO INVADE THE YOUNG REPUBLIC.

AUGUST 16, 1920: ON THE BANKS OF THE VISTULA, BEFORE THE GATES OF WARSAW.

THE REDS ARE RETREATING! VICTORY!

LONG LIVE PIŁSUDSKI!*

THE VICTOR, MARSHAL JOZEF PIŁSUDSKI,* NOT ONLY SAVES POLAND, BUT, IN SO DOING, HELPS DEFEND ALL OF WESTERN EUROPE.**

FOUR MONTHS EARLIER, ON MAY 18, A LITTLE BOY IS BORN IN WADOWICE IN THE HOME OF KAROL AND EMILIA WOJTYŁA. THEY NAME THEIR SON KAROL JOZEF.

THIS MIDDLE-CLASS COUPLE LIVES IN A TOWN 22 MILES FROM KRAKÓW. THE FATHER IS A LIEUTENANT IN THE ARMY, THE MOTHER AN EMBROIDERER. THEIR ELDEST SON, EDMOND, IS A 14-YEAR-OLD HIGH SCHOOL STUDENT.

SO YOUR EDMOND'S AS GOOD A STUDENT AS EVER?

AS ALWAYS! MUNDEK,*** GET MY SHAWL, PLEASE. IT'S CHILLY.

AND YOU KNOW, HELENA, THIS LITTLE ONE WILL BE A GREAT MAN SOME DAY!

* FOUNDER OF THE POLISH REPUBLIC (1867–1935)
** A VICTORY CALLED THE "MIRACLE OF THE VISTULA"
*** POLISH NICKNAME FOR EDMOND

1

THE FAMILY LIVES IN A BRICK BUILDING AT 2 RYNEK STREET,* FACING SAINT MARY'S CHURCH, WHERE KAROL WAS BAPTIZED.

* TODAY, 7 KOSCIELNA STREET

MUNDEK SOON LEAVES FOR KRAKÓW TO STUDY MEDICINE. AND ONE DAY I'D LIKE YOU, LOLEK,** TO BECOME A PRIEST.

** POLISH NICKNAME FOR KAROL

WATCH OUT KAROL!

GO ON, CHAMP, TIME FOR HOMEWORK NOW!

OH, LET HIM RELAX! HE'S STILL AT THE TOP OF HIS CLASS, AND IT'S SUNDAY TOMORROW!

HOORAY, KAROL!

KAROL HAS ALL KINDS OF ADVENTURES WITH HIS BEST FRIEND, JERZY KLUGER, THE SON OF A GREAT LEADER OF THE LOCAL JEWISH COMMUNITY.

EAT YOUR FILL, BOYS, BEFORE GRANDMA GETS BACK.

I'M GOING HOME, JERZY. I THINK I'VE EATEN TOO MANY CHERRIES!

LOOK, JERZY: SOON THE RIVER WILL FREEZE OVER, AND WE CAN GO SKATING.

HAVE A LOOK AT THESE ANIMAL TRACKS, KAROL.

2

AUGUST 13, 1929.

PAPA?

KAROL ... KAROL.

IT'S YOUR MOM ...

MY DARLING EMILIA ... IT'S ALL OVER. SHE'S GONE TO HEAVEN!

WHAT A TERRIBLE SHOCK FOR LITTLE KAROL. HIS MOTHER WAS ONLY 45. HIS BIG BROTHER, NOW 21, WAS FINISHING MEDICAL SCHOOL. HIS FATHER, HAVING BEEN PROMOTED TO CAPTAIN, RETIRES TO DEVOTE HIS TIME TO LOOKING AFTER HIS YOUNG SON.

HOW DIGNIFIED, HOW BRAVE! AND HE'S RAISING HIS BOY SO WELL!

AND THE CAPTAIN IS SO DEVOUT!

ALREADY UP, PAPA?!

PRAYER MEANS TALKING TO GOD—BUT IT ALSO MEANS LISTENING TO HIM. HE HAS SO MUCH TO TELL US IN THE SILENCE.

BUT COME, LET'S HAVE BREAKFAST!

TONIGHT, CAN WE READ SOME MORE OF THE BIBLE TOGETHER? IT'S FASCINATING.

OF COURSE, AND WE'LL PRAY THE ROSARY TOO!

3

5

IN SEPTEMBER 1930, KAROL ENTERS THE STATE SECONDARY SCHOOL FOR BOYS, MARCIN WADOWITA.

DON'T YOU GET TIRED OF GETTING UP SO EARLY TO GO TO MASS EVERY DAY BEFORE SCHOOL?

NOT AT ALL! MY DAD COMES WITH ME. AND I'M IN THE CHURCH CHOIR, TOO!

DO YOU WANT TO BE A PRIEST WHEN YOU GROW UP?

OF COURSE NOT! I'M GOING TO BE AN EXPLORER! I'LL TRAVEL THE WORLD!

KAROL'S BIG BROTHER, EDMOND, IS NOW A DOCTOR AT BIELSKO-BIAŁA HOSPITAL IN KRAKÓW. HE HAS MORE TIME TO VISIT HIS FATHER AND BROTHER IN WADOWICE.

IT SURE IS NICE OF YOU TO TAKE ME TO THE SOCCER GAME!

IT'LL BE GREAT! AND YOU'LL SEE BETTER UP HERE ON MY SHOULDERS!

KAROL IS A GOOD, HARDWORKING STUDENT, ALWAYS READY TO HELP OUT HIS CLASS- MATES WITH THEIR HOMEWORK. EVERYONE IS WELCOME AT HIS HOUSE. THE CAPTAIN GIVES THE CHILDREN SUPPORT AND GUIDANCE.

ENOUGH WORK FOR TODAY! HAVE A BREAK! I'LL READ YOU THE NEXT CHAPTER OF THE STORY WE STARTED LAST WEEK.

OH, YES, PLEASE! "THE DRAGON OF CASTLE WAWEL!" AND SHOW US THOSE BEAUTIFUL COLOR ILLUSTRATIONS!

ONE DAY, AS KAROL STROLLS PAST A NEIGHBOR'S HOUSE.

EXCUSE ME, SIR! THE DOOR WAS OPEN AND— OH!

WHY, IT'S LITTLE KAROL! COME IN! AS YOU SEE, WE'RE REHEARSING A PLAY. STAY, IF YOU LIKE!

4

6

AND SO HE DOES! KAROL TAKES TO THE STAGE STRAIGHTAWAY, AND SOON HE IS HOOKED! OVER THE FOLLOWING YEARS, HE BECOMES A LEADING LIGHT IN THE SCHOOL DRAMA GROUP.

DON'T YOU SEE, THE ROLE OF AN ACTOR IS LIKE THAT OF A PRIEST! THE POWER OF THE SIMPLE SPOKEN WORD CAN CHANGE HISTORY! JUST THINK, THEN, OF THE WORD OF GOD!

IT'S SETTLED! I WILL BE AN ACTOR!

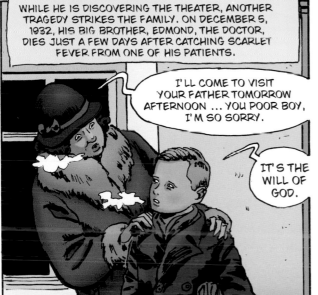

WHILE HE IS DISCOVERING THE THEATER, ANOTHER TRAGEDY STRIKES THE FAMILY. ON DECEMBER 5, 1932, HIS BIG BROTHER, EDMOND, THE DOCTOR, DIES JUST A FEW DAYS AFTER CATCHING SCARLET FEVER FROM ONE OF HIS PATIENTS.

I'LL COME TO VISIT YOUR FATHER TOMORROW AFTERNOON ... YOU POOR BOY, I'M SO SORRY.

IT'S THE WILL OF GOD.

AT SCHOOL, KAROL ASTONISHES HIS TEACHERS.

DESPITE THE FAMILY TRAGEDY, WOJTYŁA STILL GOT THE BEST GRADES THIS SEMESTER IN LATIN, GREEK, HISTORY, PHILOSOPHY, AND GERMAN!

THAT BOY WILL GO FAR!

LOLEK ENROLLS IN MORE AND MORE AFTER-SCHOOL ACTIVITIES. BESIDES THE THEATER, HE JOINS THE CONFRATERNITY OF MARY, A YOUTH GROUP DEDICATED TO PROMOTING DEVOTION TO THE BLESSED VIRGIN.

BOGUSŁAW IS ANOTHER FRIEND OF LOLEK. HIS FATHER OWNS A LITTLE RESTAURANT.

LAST NIGHT, DAD HAD TO CONFISCATE THE LOCAL POLICEMAN'S GUN AGAIN. AFTER HIS MEAL, HE'D GOTTEN SO DRUNK.

5

HERE, LOOK! STICK 'EM UP, OR I'LL SHOOT! HA, HA!

OH!

BANG

LOLEK!!

GOOD HEAVENS, BOGUSŁAW!

ANYONE HURT?

Polska bandera na północnym Atlantyku

WHEW, NO, WE'RE OKAY.

THAT WAS A CLOSE ONE! PROVIDENCE WAS WATCHING OVER THE FUTURE JOHN PAUL II!

1938: WHEN THE BISHOP OF KRAKÓW, ADAM STEPHAN SAPIEHA, VISITS HIS HIGH SCHOOL, THE PRINCIPAL ASKS KAROL TO DELIVER THE OPENING ADDRESS.

WONDERFUL! HOW SELF-ASSURED!

IT'S THE THEATRE—THAT HELPS!

APPARENTLY, THE PRINCIPAL DIDN'T HAVE TO CHANGE ONE WORD OF HIS SPEECH.

WHAT AN EXCEPTIONAL BOY! HE'D MAKE AN EXCELLENT PRIEST, DON'T YOU THINK?

IT'S NEVER EVEN CROSSED HIS MIND, BISHOP. HE WANTS TO BE AN ACTOR!

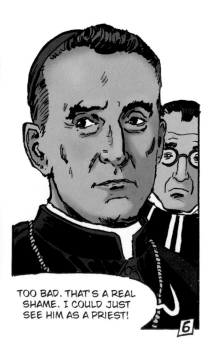

TOO BAD. THAT'S A REAL SHAME. I COULD JUST SEE HIM AS A PRIEST!

6

8

1938: ANTI-SEMITISM BEGINS TO SHOW ITS UGLY FACE IN THE COUNTRY AND AT SCHOOL. FIGHTS OFTEN BREAK OUT AMONG THE STUDENTS.

ANTI-SEMITISM IS ANTI-CHRISTIAN! ONCE YOU START HATING YOUR NEIGHBOR, WE CAN ONLY EXPECT THE WORST!

YOU'RE REALLY SURE YOU WANT TO COME WITH ME TO KRAKÓW, PAPA?

WE'LL STAY WITH YOUR AUNT STEPHANIA, MY DEAR EMILIA'S SISTER.

ON MAY 27 OF THE SAME YEAR, KAROL GRADUATES FROM HIGH SCHOOL AND ENROLLS IN THE PRESTIGIOUS JAGIELLONIAN UNIVERSITY IN KRAKÓW TO STUDY FOR A DEGREE IN LITERATURE.

DURING HIS STUDIES, HE ALSO ENROLLS IN THE KRAKÓW THEATER COMPANY. HIS FATHER IS ONE OF HIS MOST FAITHFUL FANS.

BRAVO, KAROL! A WONDERFUL PERFORMANCE! YOU'RE A GREAT ACTOR!

SEPTEMBER 1, 1939: ON THE FIRST FRIDAY OF THE MONTH, WHILE YOUNG KAROL WOJTYŁA SERVES THE MORNING MASS AT WAWEL CATHEDRAL.

GERMANY HAS JUST INVADED POLAND. WITH THAT, MASS ENDS ABRUPTLY.

BOOM WHOOOO BOOM OOSH

FATHER FIGLEWICZ, WHAT ARE THOSE SIRENS, THESE EXPLOSIONS?!

IT'S WAR, KAROL, WAR! LET US PRAY FOR OUR POOR COUNTRY!

BOOM

QUICK! DAD'S ALL ALONE AT HOME!

AND SO THE EXODUS BEGINS. MILLIONS OF REFUGEES FILL THE ROADS.

THE GERMANS! THE GERMANS!

QUICK, INTO THE DITCH!

VROOM RAT-TA-TA-TA-TAT

LET'S GO BACK TO KRAKÓW, PAPA. THE CITY IS OCCUPIED, BUT IT WILL BE EVEN WORSE IF WE RUN INTO THE RUSSIANS, WHO ARE NOW INVADING OUR COUNTRY!*

* SEPTEMBER 18, 1939: THE EASTERN INVASION BY THE RED ARMY

OH MY POOR POLAND!

SLAVS AND JEWS ALIKE—THE NAZIS WANT EITHER TO EXTERMINATE US OR TO REDUCE US TO SLAVERY. LORD, HAVE MERCY. TELL ME: WHAT MUST I DO?

HOW CAN I TAKE CARE OF MY FATHER, WHO IS SO WEAK? HOW CAN I FIND WORK AND PROVIDE FOR THE TWO OF US ...

... IN THE THEATER, PERHAPS!

8

BUT THE THEATERS WERE CLOSED BY THE OCCUPYING ARMY. KAROL IS FORCED TO WORK AS A DELIVERY MAN, THEN AS A LABORER IN A CHEMICAL FACTORY.

18° BELOW ZERO—I'M FREEZING! PUTTING VASELINE ON OUR FACES WAS A GOOD IDEA!

OFFER OUR SUFFERINGS UP TO THE LORD, JULIUSZ.* C'MON, CHIN UP!

* JULIUSZ KYDRIŃSKI, KAROL'S OLD SCHOOLMATE

TONIGHT, WE'LL GET TOGETHER WITH TADEUSZ AND DANUTA** AT YOUR PARENTS' PLACE TO REHEARSE OUR PLAY, AWAY FROM PRYING EYES.

CAREFUL— THE OVERSEER! WE'RE FORBIDDEN TO TALK!

** TADEUSZ KWIATKOWSKI AND DANUTA MICHAŁOWSKA, OTHER FRIENDS

STILL AWAKE, KAROL? WITH YOUR WORK AND YOUR REHEARSALS, YOU'LL MAKE YOURSELF ILL!

I'M FINISHING MY PLAY JEREMIAH, BASED ON THE BIBLE. I'VE SET IT IN 14TH-CENTURY POLAND. YOU'LL LIKE IT, PAPA!

FEBRUARY 18, 1941: THAT EVENING, AT THE KYDRYNSKIS'.

HERE YOU ARE, KAROL—A MEAL AND MEDICINE FOR YOUR FATHER. MARIA WILL GO WITH YOU TO HEAT UP THE FOOD.

BUT AS THEY ARRIVE...

PAPA, MARIA'S HERE!

PAPA?

OH, PAPA! OH NO!

9

11

A FEW DAYS AFTER THIS TERRIBLE TRAGEDY.

WE'RE ALL SO FOND OF YOU, KAROL. COME AND LIVE WITH US. WE'LL BE LIKE A SECOND FAMILY TO YOU.

THANKS, JULIUSZ. THIS HAS BEEN A TERRIBLE BLOW. I CAN'T GET OVER IT, EVEN IN PRAYER.

IN THE PARISH OF SAINT STANISŁAW-KOSTKA, KAROL MEETS JAN TYRANOWSKI. SINCE THE DEPORTATION OF THE SALESIAN PRIESTS,* JAN, A LAYMAN, HAS BEEN IN CHARGE OF THE SPIRITUAL WELL-BEING OF THE YOUNG.

THAT'S ENOUGH LATIN FOR TODAY, MIETEK.** YOU'RE MAKING GREAT PROGRESS. BUT IT'S TIME FOR OUR LIVING ROSARY MEETING WITH JAN.

JAN'S AMAZING. WHAT FAITH AND HOLINESS—WHAT COURAGE!

* AFTER A GESTAPO ROUNDUP, NOT A SINGLE PRIEST WAS LEFT IN THE PARISH.

** THE NICKNAME OF KAROL'S FRIEND, MIECZYSŁAW MALIŃSKI, WHOM HE MET AT JAN TYRANOWSKI'S LIVING ROSARY.

HIS TALKS ARE SO PROFOUND, AND HIS LIFESTYLE PROVES THAT YOU CAN NOT ONLY LEARN ABOUT GOD—YOU CAN LIVE WITH GOD.

THERE'S A REASON HE NAMED OUR GROUP THE "LIVING ROSARY"!

THANKS TO HIM, I'M JUST NOW GETTING TO KNOW THE AMAZING LIVES OF SAINT JOHN OF THE CROSS AND SAINT TERESA OF ÁVILA!

BUT THE THEATER REMAINS KAROL'S GREAT PASSION. IN JULY 1941, HE MEETS THE CELEBRATED ACTOR MIECZYSŁAW KOTLARCZYK AND HIS WIFE, REFUGEES IN KRAKÓW.

THE APARTMENT WHERE I USED TO LIVE WITH MY FATHER IS EMPTY. YOU AND YOUR WIFE ARE WELCOME TO MOVE IN.

I ACCEPT ON ONE CONDITION: THAT YOU MOVE IN WITH US TOO!

WITH THE CREATION OF THE RHAPSODIC THEATER,*** WE'RE ENTERING THE RESISTANCE. OUR GOAL IS TO SAVE THE CULTURE AND SOUL OF OUR COUNTRY!

*** IN ANCIENT GREECE, THE RHAPSODES WERE POETS WHO WENT FROM HOUSE TO HOUSE TO RALLY THE SPIRITS OF THE PEOPLE IN TIME OF WAR.

BE VERY CAREFUL. SOME DO BATTLE WITH GUNS—WE'RE GOING TO DO BATTLE THROUGH THE POWER OF THE WORD AND OUR CONVICTIONS.

10

KAROL CONTINUES TO WORK FOR THE CHEMICAL COMPANY. HE IS MOVED FROM THE QUARRY TO A FACTORY IN THE BOREK-FALECKI SUBURB.

YOU'VE WORKED HARD, KAROL. TAKE A BREAK. I CAN SEE YOU'RE ITCHING TO GET BACK TO YOUR BOOKS.

AN AMAZING YOUNG MAN: HARDWORKING, DEDI-CATED. I MAY BE AN OLD ATHEIST-SOCIALIST, BUT I'M REALLY MOVED WHEN I SEE HIM ON HIS KNEES FOR HOURS IN PRAYER!

YOU'RE NOT KIDDING; HE'S NOT AFRAID OF THE GERMAN OVERSEERS OR OF ANY MOCKERY. SOMETIMES EVEN THE REAL TOUGH GUYS JOIN HIM WHEN HE PRAYS, WITH TEARS IN THEIR EYES.

FALL 1942.

FATHER FIGLEWICZ,* MY MIND IS MADE UP. I WANT TO BECOME A PRIEST.

* THE ONLY PRIEST LEFT IN KAROL'S PARISH OF SAINT STANISŁAW-KOSTKA

YOU KNOW THE NAZIS HAVE FORBIDDEN THE TRAINING OF NEW PRIESTS. IT WON'T BE EASY. YOU'LL HAVE TO BE TRAINED IN SECRET, AND IT WILL MEAN A LOT OF WORK.

ONE NIGHT IN SPRING 1943.

GIVE UP THE THEATER? BUT, DON'T YOU REALIZE THAT YOU'RE MY MOST GIFTED STUDENT! YOU CAN'T BE SERIOUS!

I'LL NEVER BE AN ACTOR, MIECZYSŁAW. I'LL BE A PRIEST.

BUT YOU'RE A BORN ACTOR. YOU'LL PERFORM FOR HIGH SOCIETY ONCE PEACE IS RESTORED. AND YOU COULD WITNESS TO YOUR FAITH THROUGH INSPIRING PLAYS.

NO, MY DEAR TEACHER AND FRIEND. THERE WILL BE NO MORE PERFORMANCES FOR ME!

11.

13

FEBRUARY 29, 1944: ON THE WAY HOME FROM THE FACTORY.

I'LL GET A FEW HOURS SLEEP AND THEN GET BACK TO ARISTOTLE AND SAINT THOMAS AQUINAS. EXAMS ARE COMING UP.

AAAAAH!

AT THE HOSPITAL.

WELL, MY OLD FRIEND, YOU CERTAINLY GAVE US A SCARE!

IT SEEMS I WAS BROUGHT HERE BY A STREETCAR DRIVER AND A GERMAN OFFICER, AND I WAS IN A COMA FOR 9 HOURS. BUT I'M FEELING BETTER. THEY'RE LETTING ME OUT SOON!

KAROL IS RELEASED TO GO BACK TO WORK AT THE FACTORY AND RETURNS TO HIS STUDIES AT THE SECRET SEMINARY RUN BY ARCHBISHOP ADAM STEPHAN SAPIEHA, A BRAVE RESISTER OF THE NAZI REGIME.

A WORKER AT THE FACTORY? OKAY, MOVE ALONG.

WHEW, FOR A MOMENT I THOUGHT I WAS IN FOR THE SAME FATE AS MY FRIEND JERZY,* SHOT YESTERDAY BY THE GERMANS.

* JERZY ZACHUTA, A SEMINARIAN AND SACRISTAN

AUGUST 1, 1944: AN UPRISING IN WARSAW. THE FIGHTING IS BLOODY, AND THE REPRESSION TERRIBLE.

FREEDOM FOR POLAND!

THE CAPITAL IS RAZED TO THE GROUND BY HITLER'S PERSONAL ORDERS.

AUGUST 6, KRAKÓW: THE GESTAPO DO A SWEEP THROUGH THE TOWN TO PREVENT ANOTHER UPRISING.

THAT WAS CLOSE! I HOPE KAROL DIDN'T GET ARRESTED!

12

JUST THEN, AT KAROL'S HOME ON TYNIECKA STREET.

QUICK, HIDE IN THE YARD! THE GERMANS ARE OUTSIDE ARRESTING ALL ABLE-BODIED YOUNG MEN!

I'M STAYING! I'LL GO PRAY IN MY ROOM IN THE BASEMENT!

SCHNELL! SEARCH ALL THE ROOMS!

OVER THERE—THAT MUST BE THE BASEMENT!

NO, NO, LET'S GO UPSTAIRS!

AFTER THE RAID.

THEY'VE GONE, AND THEY DIDN'T FIND KAROL!

IT'S A MIRACLE. AND HE'S STILL PRAYING IN HIS ROOM!

THE GERMANS COULD RETURN AT ANY MOMENT. THINGS HAD BECOME TOO RISKY FOR KAROL.

TAKE THIS SHORTCUT. WE'LL AVOID THE PATROLS AND GET TO THE ARCHBISHOP'S FASTER!

AFTER CROSSING THE TOWN WITHOUT ANY DANGEROUS ENCOUNTERS.

THE COAST IS CLEAR, QUICK!

YOU'RE HERE, KAROL! GOD BE WITH YOU!

THANKS FOR EVERYTHING, IRENA. I'LL PRAY FOR ALL OF YOU! FAREWELL!

13

WELCOME, KAROL. WE'VE BEEN ANXIOUSLY AWAITING YOU. MALIŃSKI AND A FEW OF YOUR OTHER FRIENDS WILL SOON JOIN US. IN THE MEANTIME, STASZEK WILL SHOW YOU TO YOUR ROOM!

THE NEXT DAY.

GENTLEMEN, EACH OF YOU WILL RECEIVE A CASSOCK SO THAT YOU'LL LOOK LIKE PRIESTS IN CASE THE NAZIS BURST IN.

A BIT BIG, PERHAPS, BUT IT WILL DO!

YOU WILL BE SAFE HERE. YOU WILL SOON RECEIVE NEW IDENTITY PAPERS. DO NOT, UNDER ANY CIRCUMSTANCES, LEAVE THE PALACE: YOUR LIFE IS AT STAKE!

I AM YOUR RECTOR AND TAKE FULL RESPONSIBILITY FOR ALL THAT HAPPENS HERE. PRAY AND WORK! THE FREE POLAND WILL HAVE NEED OF GOOD AND HOLY PRIESTS.

AS FOR YOU, KAROL, THE GERMANS HAVE ALREADY BEEN INFORMED OF YOUR ABSENCE FROM THE FACTORY. I'LL TAKE CARE OF IT. A YOUNG MAN WHO DISAPPEARS THESE DAYS—WELL, IT'S NOT UNUSUAL, IS IT?

IN THE MEANTIME, THE RED ARMY PUSHES THE GERMANS BACK TOWARD THEIR OWN BORDERS.

14

16

THE RUSSIANS COULD BE IN KRAKÓW ANY DAY NOW.

IN THE MEANTIME, THE GERMANS ARE MORE AND MORE DANGEROUS!

BETWEEN AIDING PRISONERS AND COMFORTING FAMILIES, THE PRINCE* WILL HAVE HIS WORK CUT OUT FOR HIM— AND ON TOP OF THAT, THERE IS THE LACK OF PRIESTS IN THE PARISHES.

AND HE'S ALSO DOING HIS BEST TO ISSUE AS MANY BAPTISMAL CERTIFICATES AS POSSIBLE TO THE JEWS TO SAVE THEM FROM DEPORTATION!

THE MAN'S A SAINT! WHAT FAITH! DID YOU NOTICE HOW LONG HE PRAYS AFTER MORNING MASS AND AT EVENING MEDITATION?

* THE NAME GIVEN THE ARCHBISHOP BECAUSE OF HIS ARISTOCRATIC ORIGINS

WINTER 1944.

BA-BOOM BOOOM

?

DID YOU HEAR THAT? DON'T STAY HERE—IT'S THE RUSSIANS! QUICK, INTO THE CRYPT!

THEY'RE BOMBARDING THE FACTORIES ON THE CITY OUTSKIRTS!

ONE MORNING.

IT LOOKS LIKE THEY'RE LEAVING KRAKÓW!

YES, ALONG WITH ALL THAT THEY'VE STOLEN FROM OUR MUSEUMS!

VRROOOM

THE WEHRMACHT** WERE STILL THERE, STILL HOLDING OUT, BUT ON THE NIGHT OF JANUARY 16, 1945...

BOOOOM

TO THE SHELTERS! I'M STAYING HERE!

THEY'VE BLOWN UP THE BRIDGES!

CRASH CLANK

** THE GERMAN ARMY

IS ANYONE HURT?

15

AT BREAK OF DAY.

YOU CAN COME OUT. THE RUSSIANS ARE HERE. THE WAR IS OVER FOR YOU!

COME HAVE SOME FOOD...

...YOU MUST REALLY NEED IT!

LATER.

MARSHAL KONIEW, COMMANDER OF THE UKRAINIAN FRONT. I HAD TO COME TO PAY MY RESPECTS TO THE GREAT POLISH PATRIOT AND TO THANK HIM FOR HIS UNSWERVING OPPOSITION TO HITLER DURING THE OCCUPATION!

THE SOVIET GENERALS AND MARSHALS HAVE BEEN MEETING WITH THE PRINCE FOR DAYS NOW!

LET'S GET BUSY, MIETEK! GETTING THE SEMINARY BACK IN ORDER WILL BE QUITE AN UNDERTAKING!

WHAT A STENCH! BUT COME, COME, BE BRAVE!

AT LAST! IT'S NICE TO BE ABLE TO WALK DOWN THE STREET WITHOUT FEARING FOR ONE'S LIFE. BUT TO THINK THAT THE WAR STILL ISN'T OVER—THEY'RE STILL FIGHTING IN THE WEST. GERMANY STILL HASN'T SURRENDERED.

ARE WE REALLY FREE? THE UNIFORMS HAVE CHANGED, BUT—WE'LL SEE.

16

REGULAR CLASSES RESUME AGAIN AT THE THEOLOGY FACULTY.* KAROL COMPLETES HIS THIRD YEAR. HE SPEAKS RUSSIAN WELL AND TRIES TO GET TO KNOW THE NEW OCCUPIERS.

* JAGIELLONIAN UNIVERSITY IN KRAKÓW

YES, I REMEMBER GOING INTO A CHURCH ONCE WITH MY MOTHER WHEN I WAS A BOY. YOU KNOW, AT SCHOOL AND AT WORK, WE WERE ALWAYS TOLD THAT THERE WAS NO GOD!

BUT I ALWAYS KNEW HE EXISTED! I'D REALLY LIKE TO KNOW MORE ABOUT HIM!

GOD KNOWS YOUR HEART. I HOPE WE MEET AGAIN. I'LL PRAY FOR YOU AND YOUR COUNTRYMEN EVERY DAY.

NOW THERE'S A LESSON! NO IDEOLOGY OR GOVERNMENT CAN REMOVE GOD FROM MAN'S SPIRIT!

MAY 1945.

HITLER COMMITTED SUICIDE IN HIS BUNKER IN BERLIN.** GERMANY HAS UNCONDITIONALLY SURRENDERED,*** AND YET THE RUSSIANS ARE STILL HERE!

STALIN HAS REFUSED THE RETURN OF THE LEGAL POLISH GOVERNMENT EXILED IN LONDON. HE IS IMPOSING PUPPET RULERS ON US, AND THE WEST IS DOING NOTHING!

** APRIL 30, 1945
*** MAY 8, 1945

WE'VE BEEN BETRAYED! HALF OF EUROPE WAS HANDED OVER TO THE SOVIETS IN YALTA!****

POOR POLAND. HERE WE ARE AGAIN IN THE HANDS OF A TOTALITARIAN REGIME!*****

**** ROOSEVELT (USA), CHURCHILL (UK), AND STALIN (USSR) MET AT THE YALTA CONFERENCE IN THE CRIMEA.
***** A GOVERNMENT THAT EXERCISES TOTAL CONTROL OVER THE LIVES OF ITS PEOPLE.

CATHOLICS ARE IN THE MAJORITY—THE RUSSIANS WILL HAVE TO RECKON WITH THAT! MAY GOD HELP US WIN THIS NEW BATTLE!

WOJTEK, MY OLD FRIEND, HOW NICE TO SEE YOU AGAIN! WE HEARD YOU ARE A COM-MUNIST NOW!

EVERYONE'S GOING OVER TO THE LEFT, INCLUDING ME. BUT YOU TWO— IN CASSOCKS? YOU'RE KIDDING!

FROM BARBARISM TO ATHEISM! FROM ANTI-SEMITISM AND ETHNIC CLEANSING TO A FULL-FLEDGED CAMPAIGN AGAINST GOD!

YOU SAY EVERYONE'S GOING TO THE LEFT?

WELL, WE'RE NOT.

AND KAROL AND HIS FRIEND MALIŃSKI LAUGH AS THEY TURN RIGHT INTO A SIDE STREET. JUST ANOTHER LITTLE ACT OF RESISTANCE!

THE FUTURE POPE STARTS HIS FOURTH AND FINAL YEAR OF THEOLOGY BEFORE ORDINATION. HE WORKS AT THE SAME TIME AS AN ASSISTANT PROFES-SOR AND WONDERS ABOUT ONE DAY JOINING THE CARMELITES.

LEAD A CONTEMPLATIVE LIFE, WITHDRAWN FROM THE WORLD— HMM! FIRST FINISH WHAT YOU'VE ALREADY STARTED!

FEBRUARY 18, 1946: ARCHBISHOP SAPIEHA IS MADE A CARDINAL IN ROME.

AFTER HAVING RECEIVED BRILLIANT RESULTS ON HIS EXAMS, ON NOVEMBER 1, 1946, IN THE LITTLE CHAPEL OF THE ARCHBISHOP'S PALACE...

HERE I AM, A PRIEST OF CHRIST FOR ETERNITY, AND TOMORROW I WILL CELEBRATE MY FIRST MASS! WHAT JOY!

18

20

THE NEXT DAY, IN THE CRYPT OF WAWEL CATHEDRAL, KAROL CELEBRATES NOT JUST ONE, BUT THREE MASSES.*

DOMINUS VOBISCUM.

* ON NOVEMBER 2, THE DAY OF PRAYER FOR THE DEAD, PRIESTS ARE ALLOWED TO SAY THREE MASSES.

A FEW DAYS LATER, ON NOVEMBER 11.

WHAT A JOY FOR ME TO CELEBRATE MY FIRST BAPTISM FOR THE CHILD OF MY OLD FRIENDS FROM THE RHAPSODIC THEATER, TADEUSZ AND HALINA!

HOW MOVING FOR US, KAROL— SORRY — FATHER WOJTYŁA!

WOJTYŁA, I'VE DECIDED TO SEND YOU TO ROME FOR TWO YEARS TO COMPLETE YOUR STUDIES AT THE ANGELICUM.**

BUT, YOUR EMINENCE, IN THESE SAD TIMES, ISN'T MY PLACE RATHER AMONG MY PEOPLE?

** THE PONTIFICAL UNIVERSITY OF SAINT THOMAS AQUINAS

YOU HAVE GREAT TALENTS, AND OUR POOR POLISH CHURCH NEEDS BRILLIANT, WELL-TRAINED MEN LIKE YOU. DIFFICULT TIMES LIE AHEAD.

IN ROME, KAROL ROOMS AT THE BELGIAN COLLEGE. HIS FREE TIME IS SPENT EXPLORING THE ETERNAL CITY.

SAINT PETER'S SQUARE— HOW WONDERFUL!

AND DOWN THERE ARE THE APARTMENTS OF PIUS XII, OUR GOOD POPE PACELLI!

19

21

KAROL ALSO TRAVELS THROUGHOUT ITALY. HE VISITS SAN GIOVANNI ROTONDO AND GOES TO CONFESSION TO PADRE PIO.

DEAR LORD, WHAT A WONDERFUL MASS. WHAT SOLEMNITY! THE PADRE RELIVES EVERY MOMENT OF THE PASSION IN HIS OWN FLESH. HOW MOVING!

DURING VACATION, THE FUTURE POPE TRAVELS THROUGH FRANCE, BELGIUM, AND HOLLAND. ON JUNE 19, 1948, HE PASSES HIS DOCTORATE WITH FLYING COLORS!

I'LL FINALLY SEE MY BELOVED POLAND AGAIN, THOUGH, SADLY, SHE'S STILL SUBJECTED TO TYRANNY. THE FREE NATIONS DON'T KNOW HOW LUCKY THEY ARE!

DESPITE HIS DOCTORATE, THE YOUNG GRADUATE IS APPOINTED PARISH PRIEST OF THE POOR LITTLE COUNTRY CHURCH OF NIEGOWIĆ, 25 MILES FROM KRAKÓW.

HE'S HERE! HE'S HERE! OUR PRIEST IS HERE!

THE NEW PRIEST IS GOING DOWN ON HIS KNEES BEFORE OUR VILLAGE!

YES, LOOK AT THAT: HE LOOKS LIKE SUCH A NICE MAN!

MAY THE LORD BE PRAISED— WELCOME TO OUR VILLAGE!

MY NAME'S KAROL WOJTYŁA!

HELLO, FATHER BUZAŁA! I'M YOUR NEW ASSISTANT!

WELCOME, KAROL. I'VE BEEN EXPECTING YOU. I NEED SOMEONE YOUNG AND DYNAMIC FOR THE CHILDREN'S RELIGIOUS INSTRUCTION!

AND SO...

THERE'S NOTHING LIKE A GOOD GAME OF SOCCER AFTER CATECHISM!

WOW, WHAT A KICK!

IN ALL WEATHERS, HE CARRIES OUT HIS MISSION WITH DEDICATION.

I MUST INTRODUCE THE CHILDREN TO THE THEATER. THEY'D ENJOY THAT! AND THAT WOODEN CHURCH! IT WOULD BE GOOD TO REPLACE IT WITH A BRICK CHURCH!

DURING A VISIT FROM MALIŃSKI.

YOU SEE, MIETEK, THE SOIL IS RICH HERE BUT THE PEOPLE HAVE TROUBLE FEEDING THEMSELVES. I TAKE CARE OF THE HENS, RABBITS, AND A LITTLE VEGETABLE GARDEN.

I'M DISCOVERING HERE THE BEAUTY OF MY CALLING. IN THE CONFESSIONAL I ENCOUNTER PEOPLE IN ALL THE DEPTH OF THEIR HUMANITY!

THAT'S THE REAL CROWNING GLORY OF THE PRIESTHOOD— TO BE CHRIST TO OUR PEOPLE, BRINGING THEM THE MERCY AND GRACE OF GOD. TO DO THAT WELL, WE NEED A DEEP PRAYER LIFE.

KAROL STILL FINDS THE TIME TO WORK ON A CATHOLIC WEEKLY PAPER, *TYGODNIK POWSZECHNY.*

WONDERFUL! OUR READERS WILL BE WONDERING WHO THESE GREAT WRITERS ARE— ANDRZEJ JAWIEN AND STANISLAS ANDRZEJ GRUDA* — WHO DELIGHT THEM WITH SUCH REMARKABLE ARTICLES AND POEMS!

* THE PEN NAMES KAROL USED

MY DEAR EDITOR IN CHIEF, LET'S NOT CONFUSE THE ROLES OF PRIEST AND WRITER!

23

AFTER 8 MONTHS IN NIEGOWIĆ, FATHER WOJTILA IS APPOINTED TO THE PARISH OF SAINT FLORIAN IN KRAKÓW ON MARCH 17, 1949.

BACK TO THE CITY. WHETHER THEY ARE PEASANTS, TOWNSPEOPLE, OR ACADEMICS, THE SHEEP ARE THE SAME EVERYWHERE—THEY ALL NEED A GOOD SHEPHERD!

THE COMMUNISTS ARE PUTTING MORE AND MORE PRESSURE ON THE CHURCH!

THEY WON'T HAVE LIKED POPE PIUS XII'S APPOINTMENT OF BISHOP WYSZYŃSKI AS PRIMATE OF POLAND LAST YEAR.*

AND THEY ALSO HAVE TO DEAL WITH OUR DEAR CARDINAL SAPIEHA, WHO'S STILL AS COMBATIVE AS EVER!

TYGODNIK POWSZECNY

STEFAN WYSZYŃSKI

* NOVEMBER 12, 1948; WYŚZYNSKI WAS ALSO ARCHBISHOP OF WARSAW AND GNIEZNO.

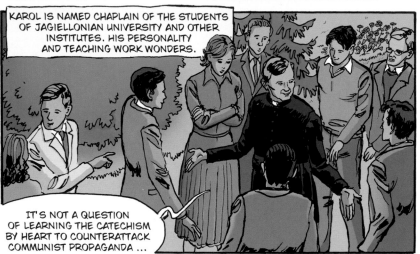

KAROL IS NAMED CHAPLAIN OF THE STUDENTS OF JAGIELLONIAN UNIVERSITY AND OTHER INSTITUTES. HIS PERSONALITY AND TEACHING WORK WONDERS.

IT'S NOT A QUESTION OF LEARNING THE CATECHISM BY HEART TO COUNTERATTACK COMMUNIST PROPAGANDA ...

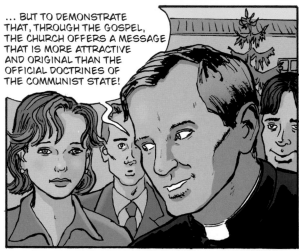

... BUT TO DEMONSTRATE THAT, THROUGH THE GOSPEL, THE CHURCH OFFERS A MESSAGE THAT IS MORE ATTRACTIVE AND ORIGINAL THAN THE OFFICIAL DOCTRINES OF THE COMMUNIST STATE!

FATHER IS NOW TEACHING US SAINT THOMAS AQUINAS' *SUMMA THEOLOGICA* IN LATIN!

AND GREGORIAN CHANT! COME JOIN OUR CHOIR—IT'S FANTASTIC!

AND HE ALSO HAS US VISITING THE SICK AND THE BLIND!

OUTINGS, HIKES, AND THE DISCOVERY OF NATURE ARE ALSO PART OF FATHER WOJTYŁA'S PROGRAM.

WE'VE ARRIVED! WE'LL CAMP HERE!

AN IDEAL SPOT TO CELEBRATE MASS! AND PLEASE, CALL ME WUJEK,* LIKE THE OTHERS!

IN WINTER, SKIING IS A GOOD WAY TO RELAX.

WUJEK SHOULD ENTER A COMPETITION! WHAT STYLE!

JUST AS CHRIST CAME TO LIVE AMONG MEN 2000 YEARS AGO, I LIKE BEING WITH YOUNG PEOPLE, AND HELPING THEM TO DISCOVER WHAT IT MEANS TO BE HUMAN AND TO OVERCOME THEIR PROBLEMS.

TRUE: A PRIEST MUST BE "ANOTHER CHRIST."

* UNCLE

WHAT A BEAUTIFUL WEATHER, MIETEK; LET'S GO RIGHT TO THE TOP OF THAT MOUTAIN!

WHEW! IF YOU INSIST!

MUCH LATER, AS NIGHT FALLS.

WE'RE LOST.

THE ONLY REFUGE FOR THE NIGHT IS THAT LITTLE VILLAGE. THEY MUST HAVE A RECTORY.

IS FATHER IN? WE'RE PRIESTS AND...

WE'RE LOST. COULD YOU PUT US UP FOR THE NIGHT?

23

I HEARD YOU! AND YOU'LL GET NOTHING FROM ME! WHAT A SHAME FOR PRIESTS TO BE WANDERING ABOUT IN THE NIGHT—AND WITHOUT CASSOCKS!

BUT...

THERE'S NO PLACE FOR YOU AND YOUR KIND HERE! A NIGHT IN THE BARN WILL DO YOU GOOD!

YOU CAN SLEEP IN THERE, AND CONSIDER YOURSELVES LUCKY THAT I DON'T INFORM YOUR BISHOP!

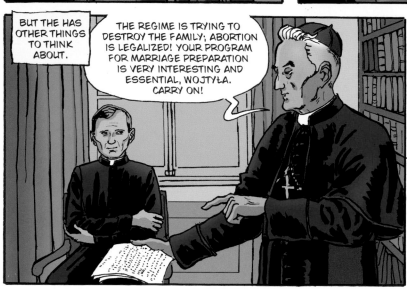

BUT THE HAS OTHER THINGS TO THINK ABOUT.

THE REGIME IS TRYING TO DESTROY THE FAMILY; ABORTION IS LEGALIZED! YOUR PROGRAM FOR MARRIAGE PREPARATION IS VERY INTERESTING AND ESSENTIAL, WOJTYŁA. CARRY ON!

BEFORE HIS DEATH ON JULY 21, 1951, THE CARDINAL APPOINTS KAROL CHAPLAIN OF HEALTH WORKERS. THE DEATH OF THE PRINCE DEEPLY AFFECTS KAROL.

THE DEAR CARDINAL WAS LIKE A SECOND FATHER TO ME. ANOTHER CHAPTER HAS ENDED.

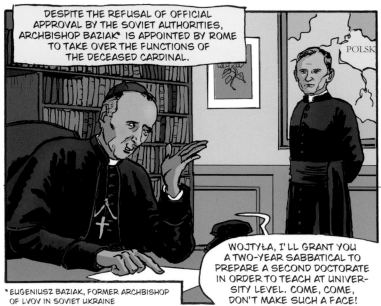

DESPITE THE REFUSAL OF OFFICIAL APPROVAL BY THE SOVIET AUTHORITIES, ARCHBISHOP BAZIAK* IS APPOINTED BY ROME TO TAKE OVER THE FUNCTIONS OF THE DECEASED CARDINAL.

POLSK

WOJTYŁA, I'LL GRANT YOU A TWO-YEAR SABBATICAL TO PREPARE A SECOND DOCTORATE IN ORDER TO TEACH AT UNIVERSITY LEVEL. COME, COME, DON'T MAKE SUCH A FACE!

* EUGENIUSZ BAZIAK, FORMER ARCHBISHOP OF LVOV IN SOVIET UKRAINE

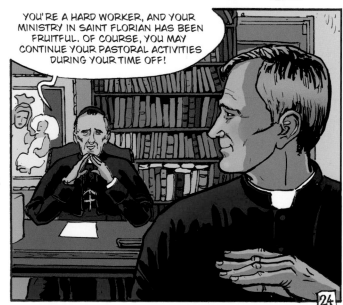

YOU'RE A HARD WORKER, AND YOUR MINISTRY IN SAINT FLORIAN HAS BEEN FRUITFUL. OF COURSE, YOU MAY CONTINUE YOUR PASTORAL ACTIVITIES DURING YOUR TIME OFF!

24

26

HIS DOCTORATE COMPLETED AS OF OCTOBER 1953, FATHER WOJTYŁA BECOMES A TEACHER AT THE KRAKÓW SEMINARY AND THE UNIVERSITY OF LUBLIN.

HUMAN RIGHTS, THE FAMILY, AND THE DEFENSE OF LIFE ARE CONSTANT THEMES OF HIS MANY LECTURES AND WRITINGS. BUT HE DOESN'T GIVE UP HIS PASTORAL CARE OF THE YOUNG.

WUJEK, ONE DAY WHEN YOU'RE POPE, YOU'LL OWE US INDULGENCES FOR HAVING MADE THIS HIKE!

WHAT NONSENSE YOU TALK!

HIS STUDENTS INTRODUCE HIM TO NEW SPORTS, WHICH HE TAKES TO WITH ENTHUSIASM.

YOU'RE RIGHT, BOYS: KAYAKING IS FANTASTIC!

AND BICYCLING TOO.

SALVE REGINA, MATER MISERICORDIAE, ♪ VITA DULCEDO... ♪♫♪♫ ♪♫♪

FACED WITH GROWING POVERTY, ANTI-CATHOLIC PERSECUTION, AND THE IMPRISONMENT OF CARDINAL WYSZYŃSKI IN THE SPRING OF 1956, THE PEOPLE OF WARSAW TAKE TO THE STREETS.

Blizej poczsna

Wobok Polsky pomocy

swoje miejsce obiekka

FREE THE CARDINAL!

BREAD AND FREEDOM!

WE WANT GOD!

IN THE FALL, THE SECRETARY-GENERAL OF THE POLISH COMMUNIST PARTY, GIVES IN AND PROPOSES A COMPROMISE.

THE RUSSIANS DIDN'T GET INVOLVED, THANK GOD!

RELIGIOUS FREEDOM IN EXCHANGE FOR POLITICAL NEUTRALITY— HMM, BE WARY!

THE CARDINAL'S BEEN FREED!

25

THE POLITICAL SITUATION LEADS FATHER WOJTYŁA TO STUDY ALL ASPECTS OF MARXISM.

THE COMMUNIST AUTHORITIES ARE TRICKED BY THIS.

SOCIALISM SEEMS TO HAVE A CERTAIN ATTRACTION FOR THIS FATHER WOJTYŁA. HE COULD BE A VALUABLE NEGOTIATING PARTNER, AND HE'S MORE FLEXIBLE THAN WYSZYŃSKI!

DON'T FORGET THAT HE WAS A WORKER IN HIS YOUNGER DAYS. LET'S KEEP AN EYE ON HIM!

DESPITE HIS UNIVERSITY CLASSES AND HIS LITERARY OUTPUT, KAROL IS ALWAYS AVAILABLE FOR HIS BELOVED STUDENTS.

YOU YOUNG PEOPLE ARE WONDERFUL BECAUSE YOU ARE GOD'S CHILDREN. ANYONE WHO TRIES TO TREAT YOU AS ANYTHING LESS DEMEANS YOU!

IN EARLY AUGUST 1956, DURING A TWO-WEEK KAYAK OUTING IN NORTHERN POLAND.

CARDINAL WYSZYŃSKI WANTS ME BACK IN WARSAW URGENTLY

GOOD NEWS, WUJEK?

I'VE BEEN APPOINTED AUXILIARY BISHOP OF KRAKÓW. BUT DON'T WORRY; I'LL BE BACK TO CELEBRATE MASS NEXT SUNDAY!

THANKS FOR COMING WITH ME, GABRIEL; AND YOU TOO, ZADISŁAW!

THERE'S A LITTLE ROAD THAT LEADS TO THE STATION. WE'LL HITCH A RIDE!

THE LOCALS AREN'T VERY HELPFUL AROUND HERE.

LET'S TRY THAT MILK TRUCK THERE!

26

28

THE TRUCK STOPS, AND THE DRIVER AGREES TO TAKE THEM TO THE STATION.

THANKS AGAIN!

BEFORE I CATCH THE TRAIN, A LITTLE MAKEOVER IS IN ORDER. I'LL BE RIGHT BACK!

POLSKI

16-10-78-JP

KOBA

TWO MINUTES LATER.

A LITTLE MORE PRESENTABLE FOR THE CARDINAL, DON'T YOU THINK?

UPON ARRIVAL IN WARSAW.

LAST JULY 4, HIS HOLINESS PIUS XII APPOINTED YOU AUXILIARY BISHOP. YOU WILL THEREFORE WORK WITH BISHOP BAZIAK!

NOW, TO PRAY! THE URSULINE CONVENT IS NEARBY. I HAVE SO MUCH TO SAY TO THE LORD!

LATER.

FATHER'S BEEN IN THE CHAPEL FOR TWO HOURS. PERHAPS I SHOULD JUST GO CHECK.

OH!

29

* CATHOLIC UNIVERSITY OF LUBLIN

WHILE HE CARRIES ON THE GOOD FIGHT IN DEFENSE OF THE FAITH.

WE MUSTN'T GIVE AN INCH TO THE COMMUNISTS. WE'LL CELEBRATE CHRISTMAS MIDNIGHT MASS OUTDOORS IN NOWA HUTA,* THE WORKERS' TOWN, SINCE THAT NEW DEVELOPMENT WAS DELIBERATELY BUILT WITHOUT A CHURCH.

A MASS FOR THE POOR, THE HUMBLE, FOR THOSE WHO HAVE NO PLACE TO GO—IT WILL BE JUST LIKE THE STABLE IN BETHLEHEM WHEN CHRIST WAS BORN.

* NEAR KRAKÓW

IN THAT SAME YEAR, 1962.

SEND THIS URGENT LETTER TO PADRE PIO IN SAN GIOVANNI ROTONDO. WITHOUT A MIRACLE, MY VERY DEAR FRIEND, THE PSYCHIATRIST WANDA POŁTAWSKA,** WILL DIE.

** LATER A MEMBER OF THE PONTIFICAL COUNCIL FOR THE FAMILY

SHE'S A 40-YEAR-OLD MOTHER OF FOUR WHO SPENT FIVE YEARS IN A GERMAN CONCENTRATION CAMP DURING THE WAR. TODAY, HER LIFE IS ENDANGERED BY CANCER.

PRAY THAT, THROUGH THE INTERCESSION OF THE BLESSED VIRGIN MARY, GOD MAY BE MERCIFUL TOWARD HER AND HER FAMILY. I AM DEEPLY GRATEFUL, THROUGH CHRIST OUR LORD, KAROL WOJTYŁA, AUXILIARY BISHOP OF KRAKÓW.

I CANNOT REFUSE HIM. ANGELINO, HOLD ONTO THIS LETTER—IT MAY BE AN IMPORTANT DOCUMENT ONE DAY.

TEN DAYS LATER.

CURED! COMPLETELY CURED! NOT A TRACE OF THE TUMOR LEFT! THANK GOD! AND THANK YOU, PADRE PIO!

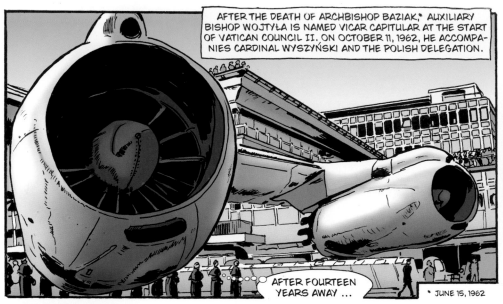

AFTER THE DEATH OF ARCHBISHOP BAZIAK,* AUXILIARY BISHOP WOJTYŁA IS NAMED VICAR CAPITULAR AT THE START OF VATICAN COUNCIL II. ON OCTOBER 11, 1962, HE ACCOMPANIES CARDINAL WYSZYŃSKI AND THE POLISH DELEGATION.

AFTER FOURTEEN YEARS AWAY ...

* JUNE 15, 1962

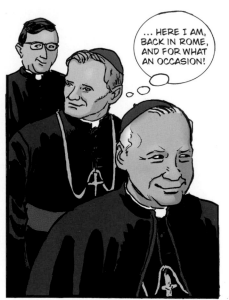

... HERE I AM, BACK IN ROME, AND FOR WHAT AN OCCASION!

WHAT A REMARKABLE YOUNG POLISH BISHOP! DID YOU HEAR HIS SPEECH THIS MORNING? HE'LL GO FAR!

FROM THE START, BISHOP WOJTYŁA STANDS OUT AMONG HIS PEERS.

DURING BREAKS ON THE MEDITERRANEAN COAST, NEAR ROME.

NOTHING LIKE A LITTLE EXERCISE TO REFRESH US AFTER THESE COUNCIL MEETINGS. HA HA!

SLOW DOWN! YOU'LL BE THE DEATH OF US!

JUNE 3, 1963: JOHN XXIII DIES. ON JUNE 22, HE IS SUCCEEDED BY CARDINAL MONTINI, WHO TAKES THE NAME PAUL VI.

ROME, JANUARY 18, 1964.

ALOSZ, DID YOU HEAR THE NEWS ON THE RADIO?! THE HOLY FATHER NAMED KAROL METROPOLITAN ARCHBISHOP OF KRAKÓW!

YES, MIETEK, AND TO THINK WE'RE STUCK HERE WITH THE COUNCIL AND OUR STUDIES, AND WE CAN'T SEE HIM BE ENTHRONED AT WAWEL CATHEDRAL IN MARCH.

THE COMMUNISTS MUST HAVE HAD TO GIVE THEIR APPROVAL?

CERTAINLY! THEY THOUGHT THAT KAROL, AT 42, WAS JUST AN INEXPERIENCED KID, AN INTELLECTUAL, A POET, A PAWN THEY COULD EASILY MANIPULATE!

30

THE COMMUNISTS SEE KAROL AS SOME KIND OF "RED" BISHOP—THE IDEAL MAN TO DIVIDE THE POLISH CHURCH HIERARCHY, SIDELINE WYSZYŃSKI, AND WEAKEN THE CHURCH'S INFLUENCE!

WELL, THEY'VE GOT THE WRONG MAN!

AND YOU, SZCZEPAN, WHAT DO YOU THINK— YOU, WHO ARE FROM KATOWICE?

I TOTALLY AGREE WITH MIETEK! AND, AS IT'S ALMOST LUNCHTIME, I PROPOSE A TOAST TO OUR NEW ARCHBISHOP, EVEN IF IT'S JUST COFFEE!

DESPITE HIS NEW POST, ARCHBISHOP WOJTYŁA PARTICIPATES IN ALL COUNCIL SESSIONS UNTIL THE LAST ONE IN DECEMBER 1965.

BREAK TIME, KAROL. COME HAVE A DRINK WITH ME!

NO TIME, MIETEK! I'M WORKING ON MY NEXT SPEECH, A TALK IN POLISH FOR VATICAN RADIO, MY LESSON PLANS, AND A BOOK!

AND HE IS ALSO ATTENTIVE TO THE PROBLEMS OF PERSECUTED CHURCHES.

IT'S OUR DUTY TO SHOW SOLIDARITY WITH OUR NEIGHBOR, THE CHURCH OF CZECHOSLOVAKIA. RIGHT HERE, WE'LL ORDAIN* THESE FUTURE PRIESTS WHO HAVE SECRETLY FLED ACROSS THE BORDER.

* ORDINATIONS WERE FORBIDDEN IN CZECHOSLOVAKIA.

ON MAY 29, 1967, HE IS INFORMED THAT THE POPE HAS ELEVATED HIM TO THE COLLEGE OF CARDINALS. KAROL—A CARDINAL AT 47!

I'LL HAVE TO CHANGE MY WARDROBE! THE CEREMONY IS ON JUNE 28. ON THE WAY TO ROME, I'LL STOP IN VIENNA TO VISIT ARCHBISHOP KÖNIG. WE HAVE A FEW IDEAS IN COMMON.

ROME, JUNE 27.

IMPOSSIBLE TO FIND A PAIR OF RED SOCKS IN THIS CITY— BUT THEY'RE INDISPENSABLE FOR A PRINCE OF THE CHURCH, YOU KNOW!

LET'S CHECK THAT STORE DOWN THERE, YOUR EMINENCE!

TURE

31

PAUL VI HAD A DEEP ADMIRATION FOR THIS YOUNG CARDINAL WHO HAD NOW BECOME THE SECOND PERSONALITY IN THE POLISH CHURCH AFTER WYSZYŃSKI.

BACK IN KRAKÓW, THE CARDINAL MANAGES TO OBTAIN PERMISSION FROM THE COMMUNIST AUTHORITIES TO BUILD A CHURCH IN NOWA HUTA. WORK BEGINS AT ONCE.

WE'VE WON, BUT THE FIGHT MUST GO ON. OTHER CHURCHES MUST SEE THE LIGHT OF DAY IN POLAND.

HE UNDERTAKES FOREIGN TRAVELS DURING 1969, FIRST TO CANADA, THEN TO THE UNITED STATES ...

... IN ORDER TO MEET THE POLISH COMMUNITIES THERE.

CARDINAL WOJTYŁA IS THE NICEST MAN I'VE EVER MET!

HE DOESN'T STAND ON CEREMONY! HE'S EVEN A LITTLE MISCHIEVOUS SOMETIMES!

DESPITE HIS MANY RESPONSIBILITIES, KAROL FINDS TIME FOR SPORTS.

HALT!

YOU'VE CROSSED THE CZECH BORDER! YOUR PAPERS!

OH GREAT! VERY WELL, THEN!

32

KAROL WOJTYŁA, CARDINAL OF KRAKÓW, AND YOU GO SKIING?!

YOU MUST TAKE US FOR IDIOTS! IT'S UNHEARD OF! WHERE DID YOU STEAL THESE PAPERS?

COME ON, FOLLOW US. YOU CAN EXPLAIN DOWN AT THE STATION!

MY APOLOGIES, YOUR EMINENCE, BUT YOU MUST ADMIT THAT IT'S A LITTLE UNUSUAL.

NOT A PROBLEM.

I ALSO PLAY SOCCER, SWIM, AND I GO KAYAKING!

WE ARE CITIZENS OF THIS COUNTRY, OF OUR CITY ...

KAROL BECOMES A CHARISMATIC PUBLIC FIGURE AND DEFENDER OF RELIGIOUS FREEDOM.

... BUT WE'RE ALSO THE PEOPLE OF GOD, BLESSED WITH OUR OWN CHRISTIAN SENSITIVITY. WE'LL GO ON DEMANDING THE RIGHTS THAT ARE CLEARLY OURS.

THE REGIME REALIZES THAT THE YOUNG CARDINAL IS NOT THE MAN THEY WERE HOPING FOR. SO, DURING A YOUTH CAMP, THEY MAKE TROUBLE FOR HIM.

SEE YOU SOON!

STATE SECURITY! IDENTITY CHECK!

AND WHAT WAS THAT BIG BLACK CAR DOING THERE TEN MINUTES AGO?

33

"THE CAR ARRIVED AND LEFT AGAIN!" HE TOLD THE SECURITY AGENT—A CLEAR, APPROPRIATE ANSWER THAT WAS NEITHER A LIE NOR A CONFESSION!

AND THEN WHAT?

AFTER CHECKING THE GROUP'S PAPERS, THESE "GENTLEMEN" FROM "SECURITY" REDOUBLED THEIR SURVEILLANCE: I WAS FOLLOWED WHEN I WENT OUT IN THE CAR.

AND THIS PLACE IS CLEARLY BUGGED WITH MICROPHONES!

THE FUTURE JOHN PAUL II OFTEN LEAVES KRAKÓW FOR ROME. AND, IN 1973, HE IS IN AUSTRALIA FOR THE EUCHARISTIC CONGRESS.

DELIGHTFUL ANIMALS!

THEN HE VISITS NEW ZEALAND, PAPUA-NEW GUINEA, AND THE PHILIPPINES.

YOUR EMINENCE, REST A LITTLE. YOU'RE ALWAYS WORKING.

MY DEAR FATHER, IT RELAXES ME TO WRITE IN MY TRAVEL DIARY!

34

IN 1976, CARDINAL WOJTYŁA PREACHES THE LENTEN RETREAT BEFORE THE ROMAN CURIA...

I COME FROM A PERSECUTED CHURCH, WHERE THE PRIVILEGE OF MAKING A RETREAT IS THE WISH OF A GREAT MANY MEN AND WOMEN.

...PRESIDED OVER BY PAUL VI.

WHEN A MAN KNEELS IN THE CONFESSIONAL BECAUSE HE HAS SINNED, AT THAT PRECISE MOMENT HE ADDS TO THE DIGNITY OF MAN.

THEN, THE FOLLOWING YEAR, ANOTHER TRIP TO THE USA FOR THE EUCHARISTIC CONGRESS IN PHILADELPHIA.

WE ARE NOW FACING THE GREATEST HISTORICAL CONFRONTATION, BETWEEN CHURCH AND ANTI-CHURCH, GOSPEL AND ANTI-GOSPEL.

DESPITE HIS GROWING RESPONSIBILITIES AND INTERNATIONAL OBLIGATIONS, KAROL REMAINS A PRIEST AND A PASTOR, CARING AND DEVOTED TO ALL.

AFTER TEN YEARS OF HARD WORK, THE CHURCH OF NOWA HUTA, THE SYMBOL OF FREEDOM, IS FINALLY COMPLETED...

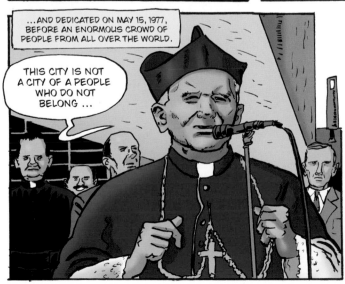

...AND DEDICATED ON MAY 15, 1977, BEFORE AN ENORMOUS CROWD OF PEOPLE FROM ALL OVER THE WORLD.

THIS CITY IS NOT A CITY OF A PEOPLE WHO DO NOT BELONG ...

... OF PEOPLE WHO CAN BE MANIPULATED ACCORDING TO THE LAWS OR RULES OF PRODUCTION AND CONSUMPTION. THIS IS A CITY OF THE CHILDREN OF GOD. THIS CHURCH HAD TO BE BUILT!

35

ON AUGUST 6, 1978, AT AGE 81, PAUL VI DIES.

HE WAS A GREAT POPE, MIETEK! THE FUNERAL WILL TAKE PLACE AUGUST 12, AND THE CONCLAVE BEGINS ON AUGUST 25!

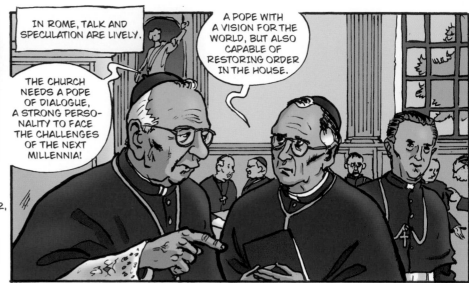

IN ROME, TALK AND SPECULATION ARE LIVELY.

THE CHURCH NEEDS A POPE OF DIALOGUE, A STRONG PERSONALITY TO FACE THE CHALLENGES OF THE NEXT MILLENNIA!

A POPE WITH A VISION FOR THE WORLD, BUT ALSO CAPABLE OF RESTORING ORDER IN THE HOUSE.

WHY NOT CONSIDER A CARDINAL FROM OUTSIDE ITALY?

YOU'RE THINKING OF CARDINAL WOJTYŁA?

AT THE POLISH COLLEGE.

DO YOU KNOW HOW MUCH TALK THERE IS ABOUT YOU, KAROL? I SAY HIS EMINENCE CARDINAL WOJTYŁA, HERE PRESENT, SHALL BE POPE!

ENOUGH OF YOUR TOMFOOLERY, MIETEK! COME FOR A DIVE IN THE POOL—THAT WILL BRING YOU TO YOUR SENSES!

THE NEXT EVENING, CARDINAL ALBINO LUCIANI, ARCHBISHOP OF VENICE, IS ELECTED POPE AND TAKES THE NAME JOHN PAUL I.

ON AUGUST 25, 111 CARDINALS FROM 38 COUNTRIES FILE INTO THE SISTINE CHAPEL, THE FUTURE POPE AMONG THEM.

36

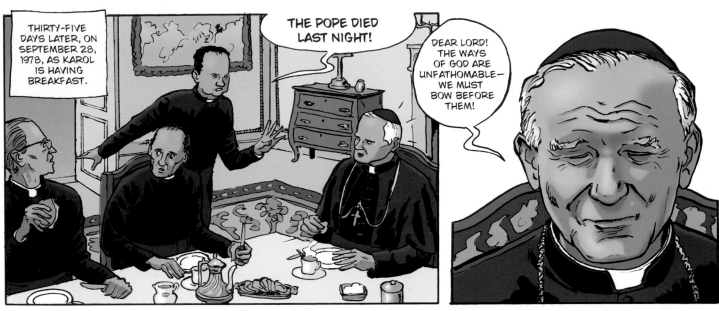

THIRTY-FIVE DAYS LATER, ON SEPTEMBER 28, 1978, AS KAROL IS HAVING BREAKFAST.

THE POPE DIED LAST NIGHT!

DEAR LORD! THE WAYS OF GOD ARE UNFATHOMABLE— WE MUST BOW BEFORE THEM!

EXCUSE ME, I'M GOING TO PRAY IN THE CHAPEL!

ON OCTOBER 3, ACCOMPANIED BY CARDINAL WYSZYŃSKI, KAROL WOJTYŁA LEAVES FOR ROME.

THE ELECTION OF A NON-ITALIAN POPE IS MORE AND MORE LIKELY.

SINCE THE COUNCIL, THE CHURCH HAS BEEN DIVIDED INTO TWO FACTIONS: TO CHOOSE SOMEONE FROM ONE SIDE WOULD INEVITABLY CAUSE PROBLEMS WITH THE OTHER.

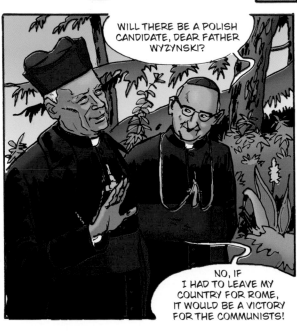

WILL THERE BE A POLISH CANDIDATE, DEAR FATHER WYZYNSKI?

NO, IF I HAD TO LEAVE MY COUNTRY FOR ROME, IT WOULD BE A VICTORY FOR THE COMMUNISTS!

NOT YOU. BUT THERE'S SOMEONE ELSE, NO?

WOJTYŁA? HE'S TOO YOUNG AND UNKNOWN!

39

THE NEW CONCLAVE BEGINS ON OCTOBER 15.

BLACK SMOKE AGAIN!

ANOTHER INCONCLUSIVE VOTE!

ON MONDAY, OCTOBER 16, AFTER THE FOURTH VOTE.

LOOK, WHITE SMOKE!

YES! WE HAVE A POPE!

HOORAH! HOORAH!

WITH THAT…

HABEMUS PAPAM! CARDINAL KAROL WOJTYŁA OF KRAKÓW HAS BEEN ELECTED POPE! HE WILL BE KNOWN AS JOHN PAUL II.*

* THE 264TH POPE OF THE CATHOLIC CHURCH

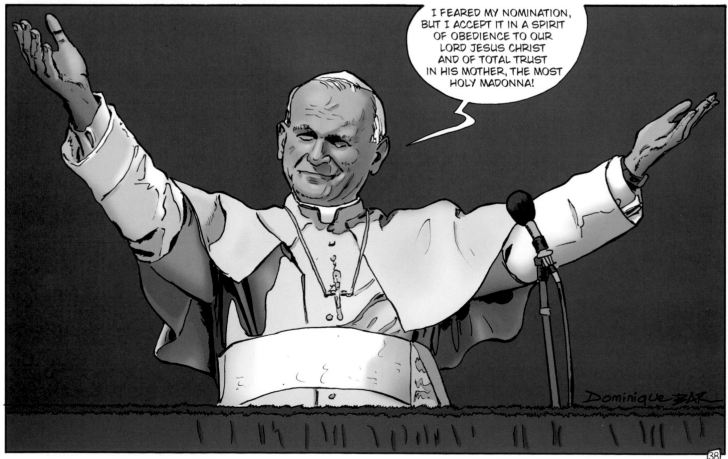

I FEARED MY NOMINATION, BUT I ACCEPT IT IN A SPIRIT OF OBEDIENCE TO OUR LORD JESUS CHRIST AND OF TOTAL TRUST IN HIS MOTHER, THE MOST HOLY MADONNA!

Dominique BAR

[38]

OCTOBER 16, 1978, SAINT PETER'S SQUARE...

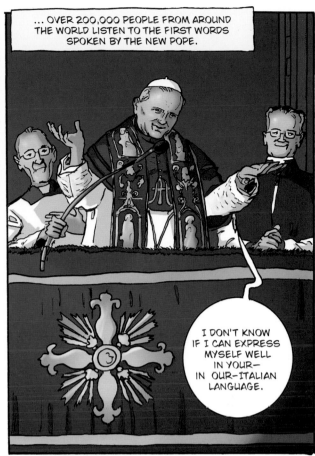

... OVER 200,000 PEOPLE FROM AROUND THE WORLD LISTEN TO THE FIRST WORDS SPOKEN BY THE NEW POPE.

I DON'T KNOW IF I CAN EXPRESS MYSELF WELL IN YOUR— IN OUR—ITALIAN LANGUAGE.

BUT IF I MAKE A MISTAKE, YOU WILL CORRECT ME!

LISTEN: HE SPEAKS ITALIAN VERY WELL!

HE'S YOUNG, CHEERFUL, AND ENERGETIC—HE'S FANTASTIC!

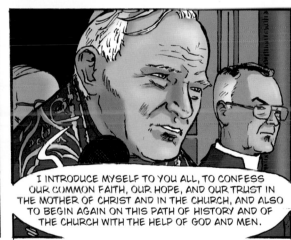

I INTRODUCE MYSELF TO YOU ALL, TO CONFESS OUR COMMON FAITH, OUR HOPE, AND OUR TRUST IN THE MOTHER OF CHRIST AND IN THE CHURCH, AND ALSO TO BEGIN AGAIN ON THIS PATH OF HISTORY AND OF THE CHURCH WITH THE HELP OF GOD AND MEN.

THE FIRST BISHOP FROM A COMMUNIST COUNTRY TO BECOME HEAD OF THE CHURCH!

WHAT WILL HE DO?

EXTRAORDINARY! A POLISH POPE—THE FIRST NON-ITALIAN POPE SINCE 1523.*

* THE DUTCH POPE ADRIAN IV (1522-1523)

WHO IS THIS KAROL WOJTYŁA? WE DON'T KNOW ANYTHING ABOUT HIM!

SURELY THIS MAN IS DESTINED TO BE A GREAT LEADER IN THE CHURCH AND IN THE WORLD.

THE POLISH PEOPLE ARE OVERJOYED.

LONG LIVE OUR POPE!

LONG LIVE JOHN PAUL II!

LONG LIVE KAROL!

WHAT A HOPEFUL SIGN FOR OUR CHURCH, PERSECUTED FOR SO LONG!

HABEMUS PAPAM!

HABEMUS PAPAM!

IN WARSAW, THE COMMUNIST LEADERS WONDER.

LONG LIVE JOHN PAUL II!

IT'S QUITE A VICTORY FOR POLISH NATIONALISM!

THE CIA* IS SURELY MIXED UP IN ALL OF THIS! MOSCOW WANTS A DETAILED REPORT ON HOW WOJTYŁA WAS ELECTED!

* CENTRAL INTELLIGENCE AGENCY (USA)

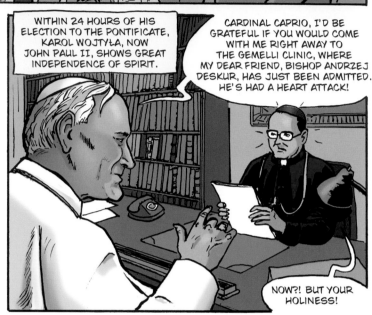

WITHIN 24 HOURS OF HIS ELECTION TO THE PONTIFICATE, KAROL WOJTYŁA, NOW JOHN PAUL II, SHOWS GREAT INDEPENDENCE OF SPIRIT.

CARDINAL CAPRIO, I'D BE GRATEFUL IF YOU WOULD COME WITH ME RIGHT AWAY TO THE GEMELLI CLINIC, WHERE MY DEAR FRIEND, BISHOP ANDRZEJ DESKUR, HAS JUST BEEN ADMITTED. HE'S HAD A HEART ATTACK!

NOW?! BUT YOUR HOLINESS!

LOOK! IT'S THE HOLY FATHER!

IT'S THE POPE!

VIVA LA PAPA!

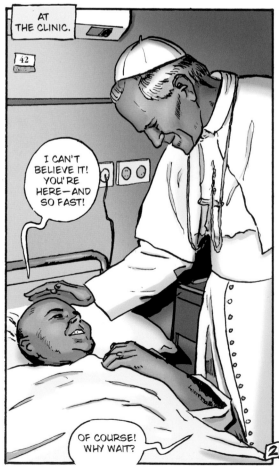

AT THE CLINIC.

42

I CAN'T BELIEVE IT! YOU'RE HERE—AND SO FAST!

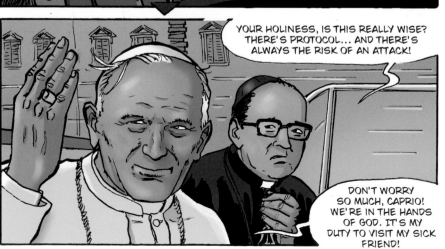

YOUR HOLINESS, IS THIS REALLY WISE? THERE'S PROTOCOL... AND THERE'S ALWAYS THE RISK OF AN ATTACK!

DON'T WORRY SO MUCH, CAPRIO! WE'RE IN THE HANDS OF GOD. IT'S MY DUTY TO VISIT MY SICK FRIEND!

OF COURSE! WHY WAIT?

2

AS HE LEAVES, 15 MINUTES LATER.

I THANK GOD FOR HAVING MET YOU!

YES, CARDINAL?

JUST A MOMENT: CARDINAL CAPRIO REMINDS ME THAT I MUST GIVE YOU A BLESSING. HE'S TEACHING ME HOW TO BE A POPE!

GOOD NIGHT, EVERYONE! MAY GOD PROTECT YOU!

ON OCTOBER 21, JOHN PAUL II HOLDS AN AUDIENCE FOR 1,500 JOURNALISTS. AFTER THE PRESS CONFERENCE, HE ANSWERS EACH JOURNALIST'S QUESTION, OFTEN IN THEIR OWN LANGUAGE.

WILL YOU CONTINUE SKIING?

THAT SEEMS UNLIKELY.

WILL YOU VISIT POLAND?

WHENEVER POSSIBLE.

THE PRESS IS DELIGHTED BY HIS SIMPLICITY.

BEFORE THE INAUGURAL MASS, WHEN HE WILL BE OFFICIALLY PROCLAIMED HEAD OF THE CHURCH, THE CARDINALS FILE TOWARD HIM FOR THE OATH OF FIDELITY.

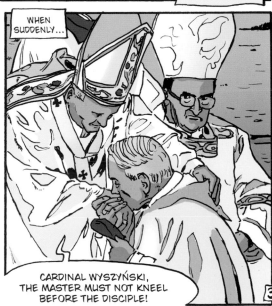

WHEN SUDDENLY...

CARDINAL WYSZYŃSKI, THE MASTER MUST NOT KNEEL BEFORE THE DISCIPLE!

③

43

MASS IS CELEBRATED BEFORE NUMEROUS DIGNITARIES AND HEADS OF STATE* FROM AROUND THE WORLD.

BROTHERS AND SISTERS, DO NOT BE AFRAID TO WELCOME CHRIST AND ACCEPT HIS POWER. HELP THE POPE AND ALL THOSE WHO WISH TO SERVE CHRIST AND, WITH CHRIST'S POWER, TO SERVE THE HUMAN PERSON ...

A GESTURE THAT MOVES ALL PRESENT.

* INCLUDING THE KING AND QUEEN OF SPAIN AND THE ARCHBISHOP OF CANTERBURY, HEAD OF THE ANGLICAN CHURCH

DO NOT BE AFRAID. OPEN WIDE THE BOUNDARIES OF STATES, ECONOMIC AND POLITICAL SYSTEMS, THE VAST FIELDS OF CULTURE, CIVILIZATION, AND DEVELOPMENT!

DO NOT BE AFRAID. CHRIST KNOWS WHAT IS IN THE HEART OF MAN. HE ALONE KNOWS IT.

AFTER RECITING THE ANGELUS.

AFTER MASS, JOHN PAUL II UNEXPECTEDLY WALKS DOWN INTO SAINT PETER'S SQUARE.

IT'S NOW TIME FOR EVERYONE TO GO HAVE LUNCH—THE POPE INCLUDED!

THE CEREMONY HAD LASTED MORE THAN FOUR HOURS.

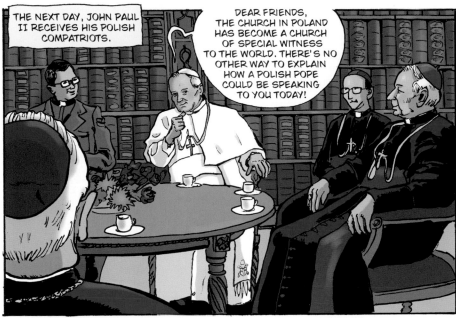

THE NEXT DAY, JOHN PAUL II RECEIVES HIS POLISH COMPATRIOTS.

DEAR FRIENDS, THE CHURCH IN POLAND HAS BECOME A CHURCH OF SPECIAL WITNESS TO THE WORLD. THERE'S NO OTHER WAY TO EXPLAIN HOW A POLISH POPE COULD BE SPEAKING TO YOU TODAY!

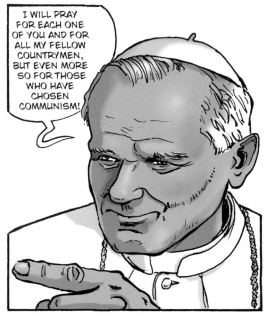

I WILL PRAY FOR EACH ONE OF YOU AND FOR ALL MY FELLOW COUNTRYMEN, BUT EVEN MORE SO FOR THOSE WHO HAVE CHOSEN COMMUNISM!

HOPE IS REKINDLED FOR ALL THOSE PERSECUTED FOR THEIR FAITH THROUGHOUT THE WORLD.

HOLY FATHER, IT IS TO THE HONOR OF THE POLISH PEOPLE THAT YOU HAVE OFFERED US IN THE REST OF THE WORLD THE GREEN SHOOTS OF HOPE...*

* FATHER CALCIU-DUMITREASA, ROMANIAN ORTHODOX PRIEST AND POLITICAL DISSIDENT

IN MOSCOW, THE KGB** SPECULATE.

BUT HOW CAN A CITIZEN OF A SOCIALIST COUNTRY HAVE BEEN ELECTED POPE?

HMM! THIS ELECTION IS CLEARLY A PLOT TO DESTABILIZE POLAND—THE FIRST STEP TOWARD THE COLLAPSE OF THE WARSAW PACT!***

** SOVIET INTERNAL SECURITY SERVICE
*** SIGNED IN WARSAW, POLAND, THIS PACT FORMED A MILITARY ALLIANCE BETWEEN THE SOVIET UNION, ALBANIA, POLAND, ROMANIA, HUNGARY, EAST GERMANY, CZECHOSLOVAKIA, AND BULGARIA.

AT THE COMMUNIST PARTY CENTRAL COMMITTEE.

WE CAN NOW EXPECT INCREASED PRESSURE FROM THE VATICAN IN FAVOR OF RELIGIOUS FREEDOM.

SO, COMRADES, LET'S WARN ROME THAT ANY LARGE-SCALE HUMAN RIGHTS CAMPAIGN WILL ONLY LEAD TO INCREASED REPRESSION OF CENTRAL AND EASTERN EUROPEAN CHURCHES.

AS FOR JOHN PAUL II, HE IS COMPLETELY AT EASE IN HIS NEW POSITION. 5 POLISH SISTERS OF THE CONGREGATION OF THE SACRED HEART OF JESUS MANAGE HIS HOUSEHOLD—SEEING TO EVERYTHING SO AS TO MAKE HIM FEEL AT HOME.

SISTER, SOME ITALIANS ARE COMING FOR LUNCH TOMORROW. I COUNT ON YOU TO DELIGHT THEM WITH ONE OF YOUR POLISH SPECIALTIES!

5

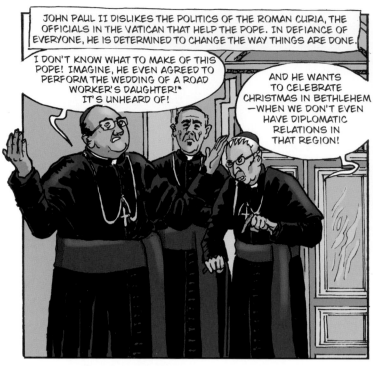

JOHN PAUL II DISLIKES THE POLITICS OF THE ROMAN CURIA, THE OFFICIALS IN THE VATICAN THAT HELP THE POPE. IN DEFIANCE OF EVERYONE, HE IS DETERMINED TO CHANGE THE WAY THINGS ARE DONE.

I DON'T KNOW WHAT TO MAKE OF THIS POPE! IMAGINE, HE EVEN AGREED TO PERFORM THE WEDDING OF A ROAD WORKER'S DAUGHTER!* IT'S UNHEARD OF!

AND HE WANTS TO CELEBRATE CHRISTMAS IN BETHLEHEM —WHEN WE DON'T EVEN HAVE DIPLOMATIC RELATIONS IN THAT REGION!

* CELEBRATED ON FEBRUARY 25, 1979, IN THE VATICAN PAULINE CHAPEL

DESPITE CONSTANT ACTIVITY, HE PRAYS OFTEN.

THE HOLY FATHER ISN'T IN HIS APARTMENTS! DO YOU KNOW WHERE I MIGHT FIND HIM? IT'S URGENT!

TRY THE CHAPEL, FATHER MAGEE!*

* A PAPAL SECRETARY

OH!

WHATEVER THE PROBLEM, IT IS CONSIDERED WHILE KNEELING BEFORE THE BLESSED SACRAMENT.

LIKE ALL SOVEREIGN PONTIFFS, JOHN PAUL II HAS HIS PERSONAL COAT OF ARMS. HE WISHED TO KEEP THOSE HE HAD AS A BISHOP.

A CAPITAL "M" BELOW A CROSS REPRESENTS MARY BENEATH THE CROSS OF CHRIST, WITH THE MOTTO *TOTUS TUUS* —"TOTALLY YOURS" — TAKEN FROM SAINT LOUIS DE MONTFORT'S PRAYER OF CONSECRATION TO JESUS THROUGH MARY.

JUST AS DURING HIS MINISTRY IN POLAND, HE DOES NOT FORGET HIS "DEAR YOUNG PEOPLE," THE HOPE OF THE CHURCH.

YOU SHOULD HAVE COME WITH US YESTERDAY.* 15,000 WENT TO HEAR HIM. HE SAID THAT HE'S COUNTING ON US AND THAT WE MUSTN'T LET HIM DOWN!

AT LEAST HE UNDERSTANDS US!

HE'S SO DYNAMIC—SUCH GOODNESS!

* NOVEMBER 29, 1978

BUT WHAT GREAT FIRMNESS AND DETERMINATION, TOO, ABOUT THE PROJECTS CLOSE TO HIS HEART. AT THE 30TH ANNIVERSARY OF THE UNIVERSAL DECLARATION OF HUMAN RIGHTS...*

FREEDOM OF RELIGION FOR ALL MUST BE RESPECTED EVERYWHERE AND BY EVERYONE.

* DECEMBER 11, 1978

IN A SPEECH TO THE DIPLOMATIC CORPS...

THE CHURCH MUST AFFIRM ITS MISSION IN THE WORLD, WITHOUT DOUBTS OR COMPLACENCY!

IN EARLY 1979, JOHN PAUL II'S FIRST DIPLOMATIC EFFORT IS A SUCCESS.

CHILE AND ARGENTINA HAVE FINALLY ACCEPTED OUR MEDIATION. IT WOULD HAVE BEEN ABSURD FOR 2 CATHOLIC COUNTRIES TO GO TO WAR.

THIS CONFLICT BROKE OUT IN 1978. BOTH STATES CLAIMED OWNERSHIP OF THE BEAGLE CHANNEL AND THE ISLANDS NORTH OF CAPE HORN. THANKS TO JOHN PAUL II, A PEACE TREATY, APPROVED BY REFERENDUM, WAS SIGNED IN 1984.

MY DEAR BROTHERS AND SISTERS, LET US PRAY ESPECIALLY FOR THE HOLY FATHER, WHO WILL SOON BE FLYING TO MEXICO.*

* MEXICO, THE BAHAMAS, AND THE DOMINICAN REPUBLIC: JANUARY 25-FEBRUARY 1, 1979

IT'S AN IMPORTANT AND DIFFICULT TRIP. THE MEXICAN GOVERNMENT IS VERY ANTICLERICAL AND HAS NO DIPLOMATIC RELATIONS WITH THE VATICAN.

EARLIER THIS CENTURY, IT HARSHLY PERSECUTED THE CHURCH.

THE PEOPLE ARE HUNGRY FOR TRUE EVANGELIZATION, BUT THE HOLY FATHER WILL SURELY HAVE TO DEAL WITH THE PROBLEMS CREATED BY LIBERATION THEOLOGY, UNFORTUNATELY SO POPULAR IN SOME OF OUR UNIVERSITIES.

A THEOLOGY TOO CLOSE TO MARXISM THAT CALLS FOR VIOLENT REVOLUTION TO CREATE A HEAVEN ON EARTH.

7

47

THE FIRST LEG OF AN IMPRESSIVE JOURNEY.

AS IS NOW HIS CUSTOM, THE HOLY FATHER KISSES THE GROUND OF EACH COUNTRY HE VISITS.

HIS TRIP TO MEXICO IS A SUCCESS. IN PUEBLA, HE SPEAKS BEFORE THE ASSEMBLY OF BISHOPS GATHERED FOR THE GREAT LATIN AMERICAN EPISCOPAL CONFERENCE.

THE CONCEPTION OF CHRIST AS A POLITICAL FIGURE, A REVOLUTIONARY POLITICIAN, AS THE SUBVERSIVE OF NAZARETH, DOES NOT TALLY WITH THE CHURCH'S FAITH.

THE NEXT DAY IN OAXACA,* MORE THAN A HALF MILLION NATIVE AMERICANS HANG ON HIS EVERY WORD.

THE POPE WISHES TO BE IN SOLIDARITY WITH YOUR CAUSE, WHICH IS THE CAUSE OF HUMBLE PEOPLE, OF THE POOR.

* 300 MILES FROM MEXICO CITY

TO BE YOUR VOICE, THE VOICE OF THOSE WHO CANNOT SPEAK OR WHO ARE SILENCED ...

... IN ORDER TO BE THE CONSCIENCE OF CONSCIENCES, AN INVITATION TO ACTION.

AS SOON AS THE POPE RETURNS, ANOTHER TRIP IS PLANNED. AND WHAT A TRIP!

IT'S CONFIRMED: THE HOLY FATHER WILL VISIT US NEXT JUNE!

WE KNEW HE'D COME BACK TO HIS OLD COUNTRY! WHAT JOY, WHAT HAPPINESS! IN MY PARISH, WE'RE ALREADY BUSY PREPARING!

THIS WON'T PLEASE EVERYONE. IMAGINE WHAT OUR DEAR LEADERS AND THE SOVIETS WILL HAVE TO SAY!

8

48

PRESSURE IS IMMEDIATELY PUT ON THE POLISH GOVERNMENT.

BUT COMRADE BREZHNEV,* GIVEN THE CIRCUMSTANCES AND INTERNATIONAL OPINION, I CAN'T OPPOSE JOHN PAUL II'S VISIT.

* FIRST SECRETARY OF THE SOVIET COMMUNIST PARTY

SO BE IT, COMRADE GIEREK,* BUT BE CAREFUL, OR YOU'LL REGRET IT!

* FIRST SECRETARY OF THE POLISH COMMUNIST PARTY

THE TRIP WOULD SHAKE COMMUNIST CONFIDENCE FOR GOOD. ON THE VERY FIRST DAY IN WARSAW, BEFORE MORE THAN 300,000 PEOPLE ...

THE EXCLUSION OF CHRIST FROM THE HISTORY OF MAN IS AN ACT AGAINST MAN!

THE PILGRIMAGE CONTINUES TO CZĘSTOCHOWA AND TO THE JASNA GÓRA SHRINE, WHICH HOUSES THE BLACK MADONNA ICON.

CAŁY TWOJ

HOW COULD I NOT VISIT THIS SHRINE OF GREAT HOPE—I WHO HAVE SO MANY TIMES WHISPERED TOTUS TUUS BEFORE THE IMAGE OF MARY.

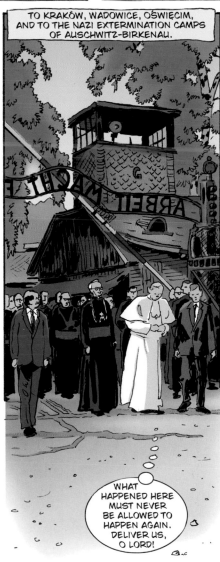

TO KRAKÓW, WADOWICE, OŚWIĘCIM, AND TO THE NAZI EXTERMINATION CAMPS OF AUSCHWITZ-BIRKENAU.

WHAT HAPPENED HERE MUST NEVER BE ALLOWED TO HAPPEN AGAIN. DELIVER US, O LORD!

RODZINA WOJTYŁÓW IK

IN KRAKÓW, JOHN PAUL II TAKES THE OPPORTUNITY TO PRAY AT HIS FAMILY'S GRAVE IN THE RADOWICE CEMETERY.

AT THE END OF THE TRIP, 13 MILLION POLES—MORE THAN A THIRD OF THE POPULATION—HAVE SEEN THE POPE IN PERSON. ALMOST ALL OTHERS HAVE SEEN OR HEARD HIM ON TV OR ON THE RADIO.

LONG LIVE POPE JOHN PAUL II

LONG LIVE POPE JOHN PAUL II

HE'LL BE BACK SOON!

IN NINE DAYS, HE'S PLANTED THE SEEDS OF A PEACEFUL REVOLUTION!

A FEW MONTHS LATER, DURING A VISIT TO THE DOLOMITES: AFTER THE BLESSING OF A STATUE OF THE VIRGIN AT OVER A 10,000-FOOT ALTITUDE.

UNFORTUN— ATELY, THAT'S DIFFICULT FOR ME IN MY PRESENT POSITION. BUT JUST BEING HERE GIVES ME A LITTLE TASTE OF THE JOY OF SKIING!

THE LAST TIME I PUT ON SKIS WAS IN THE MOUNTAINS NEAR ROME JUST A FEW MONTHS BEFORE MY ELECTION. HOW TEMPTING: I'D LOVE TO HAVE ANOTHER GO!

BUT JOHN PAUL II IS STILL VERY ATHLETIC. AS SOON AS HE RISES AT 5:30 A.M., HE DOES WEIGHTLIFTING.

DEPENDING ON THE WEATHER, HE'LL TAKE A WALK IN THE VATICAN GARDENS OR USE AN INDOOR EXERCISE BIKE.

AT CASTEL GANDOLFO.*

HOW NICE IT WOULD BE IN THIS HEAT TO DIVE INTO THAT LAKE! BUT, ALAS, I MUST KEEP OUT OF SIGHT THESE DAYS AND MAKE DO WITH THE INDOOR POOL!

* THE PAPAL SUMMER RESIDENCE

LOOK AT THEM CANOEING ON THE LAKE. I USED TO ENJOY THAT SPORT MYSELF!*

10

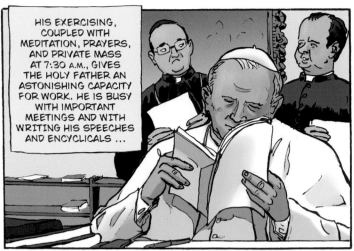

HIS EXERCISING, COUPLED WITH MEDITATION, PRAYERS, AND PRIVATE MASS AT 7:30 A.M., GIVES THE HOLY FATHER AN ASTONISHING CAPACITY FOR WORK. HE IS BUSY WITH IMPORTANT MEETINGS AND WITH WRITING HIS SPEECHES AND ENCYCLICALS ...

... AS WELL AS WITH AUDIENCES.

HIS DAY ENDS AROUND 11:00 P.M. THE LIGHTS IN THE PONTIFICAL APARTMENTS ARE ALWAYS OUT BEFORE MIDNIGHT, EXCEPT FOR CHRISTMAS AND EASTER.

FROM SEPTEMBER 29 TO OCTOBER 8, 1979, HE VISITS THE UNITED STATES, AFTER A STOP-OVER IN IRELAND, A COUNTRY BLOODIED BY ALL-TOO-FREQUENT CLASHES BETWEEN CATHOLICS AND PROTESTANTS.

IN DROGHEDA, NEAR BRITISH NORTHERN IRELAND.

FURTHER VIOLENCE IN IRELAND WILL ONLY DRAG DOWN TO RUIN THE LAND YOU CLAIM TO LOVE AND THE VALUES YOU CLAIM TO CHERISH.

NEW YORK, AT THE HEADQUARTERS OF THE UNITED NATIONS.

THE SPIRIT OF WAR SPRINGS UP AND GROWS TO MATURITY WHERE THE INALIENABLE RIGHTS OF MAN ARE VIOLATED.

AND, LATER ...

REMARKABLE! WHAT A DARING CRITICISM OF THE SOVIET SYSTEM WITHOUT ONCE UTTERING THE WORDS "COMMUNISM" OR "MARXISM."

THE DELEGATES FROM POLAND AND THE SOVIET UNION UNDERSTOOD IT! THEY LOOK A BIT WORRIED!

IF ONLY EVERYONE WOULD ENDORSE THE HOLY FATHER'S MESSAGE! IMAGINE IF HUMAN RIGHTS WERE RESPECTED EVERYWHERE.

AT THE END OF THE 5-DAY PILGRIMAGE, THE AMERICAN PRESS IS ENTHRALLED AND CANNOT PRAISE HIM ENOUGH.

John-Paul II Superstar!

IN MOSCOW, THE REACTIONS ARE INSTANT!

EVERY EFFORT MUST BE MADE TO COUNTERACT CURRENT VATICAN POLICY!

AS FOR THE KGB, IT IS FREE TO PROVE THAT THE DIRECTION TAKEN BY THE NEW POPE IS DANGEROUS FOR THE CATHOLIC CHURCH ITSELF.

TWO WEEKS LATER, FOLLOWING THE ANNOUNCEMENT OF THE POPE'S VISIT TO TURKEY, THE ISTANBUL NEWSPAPER *MILLIYET* RECEIVES A VERY ODD LETTER ...

A FANATIC BY THE NAME OF MEHMET ALI AGCA THREATENS TO KILL THE POPE IF HE DOESN'T CANCEL HIS VISIT.

HE SAYS HE'S ESCAPED FROM PRISON, WHERE HE WAS JAILED FOR MURDER. HE CLAIMS THE POPE'S VISIT IS THE BEGINNING OF ANOTHER CRUSADE AGAINST ISLAMIC NATIONS!

LET'S WARN THE POLICE AT ONCE!

12

DESPITE THE THREAT, FROM NOVEMBER 28 TO 29, JOHN PAUL II VISITS ANKARA AND THEN ISTANBUL.

FULL COMMUNION WITH THE ORTHODOX CHURCH IS A FUNDAMENTAL STEP TOWARD CHRISTIAN UNITY.

THE FOLLOWING YEAR, AFRICA RECEIVES THE HOLY FATHER FROM MAY 2 TO 12.

YOU HAVE GREAT RESOURCES. RESIST OUTSIDE INFLUENCES THAT WOULD DRAIN YOUR TRADITIONS OF THEIR MEANING!

WHAT HEAT! HE'LL KILL US AT THIS PACE!

LOOK AT HIM! HE LOOKS AS LIVELY AS HE DID WHEN WE LEFT ROME!

DON'T WORRY, MY BROTHERS: WE WILL SPEND CHRISTMAS IN THE SNOW AT TERMINILLO!*

* A FAMOUS SKI RESORT IN THE ITALIAN ABRUZZO REGION

OUR TRAVELING POPE AGAIN VISITS FRANCE, FROM MAY 30 TO JUNE 30. AT LE BOURGET AIRPORT, DURING A SUNDAY HOMILY BEFORE 250,000 PEOPLE...

FRANCE, ELDEST DAUGHTER OF THE CHURCH AND EDUCATOR OF THE PEOPLES, ARE YOU FAITHFUL TO THE PROMISES OF YOUR BAPTISM?

AT THE CARMELITE MONASTERY IN LISIEUX, HE SPENDS A LONG TIME IN PRAYER IN THE ROOM WHERE LITTLE THÉRÈSE** DIED.

** SAINT THÉRÈSE, KNOWN AS THE LITTLE FLOWER, IS A PATRON OF MISSIONS AND OF FRANCE.

13

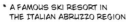

HE THEN VISITS BRAZIL FROM JUNE 30 TO JULY 12.

CLASS WARFARE CAN NEVER BRING HAPPINESS TO ANYONE. HAPPINESS CAN ONLY BE OBTAINED THROUGH THE PEACEFUL STRUGGLE FOR SOCIAL JUSTICE AS TAUGHT BY THE CHURCH!

IN JULY, POLAND IS ON THE RISE. THE PEOPLE PROTEST MASSIVE HIKES IN THE COST OF LIVING—ESPECIALLY IN GDAŃSK.*

FREEDOM!

STOP PRICE HIKES!

THE RIGHT TO STRIKE!

* THE FORMER BALTIC SEAPORT OF DANZIG.

LECH WAŁĘSA, A 36-YEAR-OLD ELECTRICIAN, BECOMES THE WORKERS' SPOKESMAN. HE DEMANDS A FREE TRADE UNION.

SOLIDARNOŚĆ

WE'LL CONTINUE TO STRIKE THROUGH SOLIDARITY!

"SOLIDARITY" WAS THE PERFECT NAME FOR THE NEW UNION!

FACED WITH THE STRIKERS' DETERMINATION AND THE SUPPORT OF THE GREAT MAJORITY OF THE BISHOPS, THE POLISH GOVERNMENT BACKS DOWN. ON SEPTEMBER 21, 1980 …

KYRIE ELEISON…

HENRYK, COME LISTEN! THEY'RE BROADCASTING THE MASS ON THE RADIO!

BUT THE SITUATION WORSENS DURING AUTUMN 1980.

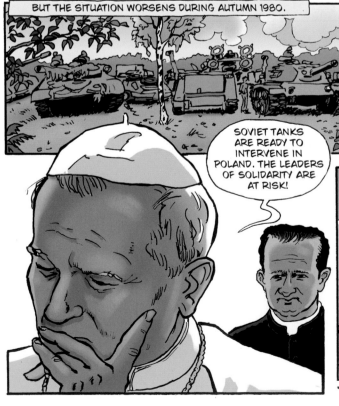

SOVIET TANKS ARE READY TO INTERVENE IN POLAND. THE LEADERS OF SOLIDARITY ARE AT RISK!

THE UNITED STATES HAS WARNED THE KREMLIN. AT ALL COSTS, THERE MUST NOT BE ANY BLOODSHED! I'LL WRITE TO LEONID BREZHNEV!**

** PRESIDENT OF THE SOVIET SUPREME COUNCIL

14

PEACE IS PRESERVED, BUT TENSIONS REMAIN. GENERAL JARUZELSKI, POLISH MINISTER OF DEFENSE, IS NAMED PRIME MINISTER ON FEBRUARY 13, 1981; A HEAVY TASK AWAITS HIM.

JOHN PAUL II CONTINUES HIS TRAVELS. ON TO GERMANY, THE COUNTRY OF LUTHER.

THERE CAN BE NO UNITY BETWEEN CATHOLICS AND PROTESTANTS WITHOUT A CHANGE OF HEART.

BEFORE UNDERTAKING A MAJOR TOUR OF ASIA, TO EVERYONE'S SURPRISE, THE HOLY FATHER APPOINTS THE YOUNG BISHOP OF ORLÉANS, JEAN-MARIE LUSTIGER, ARCHBISHOP OF PARIS.*

ME? THE SON OF POLISH JEWS?!

YOU ARE THE RESULT OF THE POPE'S PRAYERS!

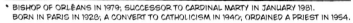

* BISHOP OF ORLÉANS IN 1979; SUCCESSOR TO CARDINAL MARTY IN JANUARY 1981. BORN IN PARIS IN 1928; A CONVERT TO CATHOLICISM IN 1940; ORDAINED A PRIEST IN 1954.

A 1800-MILE PILGRIMAGE THROUGH ASIA: THE PHILIPPINES, JAPAN, AND A RTETURN VIA ALASKA.

WE'VE JUST PASSED THE INTERNATIONAL DATELINE. SO WE'VE GAINED A DAY GOING THIS WAY. NOW, HOW SHALL WE DECIDE HOW TO SPEND THIS EXTRA DAY!

ROME, MAY 13, 1981: A MAN IN HIS TWENTIES LEAVES A LITTLE HOTEL NEAR THE VATICAN.

AT SAINT PETER'S SQUARE, HE MINGLES WITH THE CROWD AWAITING THE ARRIVAL OF THE PONTIFE.

LOOK! HE'S COMING!

VIVA IL PAPA!

5:10 P.M.

5:13 P.M.

BANG! BANG!

THE POPE'S BEEN SHOT!

A DOCTOR! AN AMBULANCE! QUICK!

THE GUNMAN HAS BEEN ARRESTED!

JOHN PAUL II IS RUSHED TO THE GEMELLI CLINIC. AROUND 12:45 A.M. THAT NIGHT...

THE HOLY FATHER WAS SERIOUSLY INJURED IN THE ABDOMEN. THE 5-HOUR OPERATION WENT WELL. THE HOLY FATHER'S CONDITION IS NOW SATISFACTORY.*

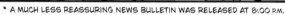

* A MUCH LESS REASSURING NEWS BULLETIN WAS RELEASED AT 8:00 P.M.

THE NEWS STUNS THE WHOLE WORLD.

HOLY MARY, PROTECT THE HOLY FATHER!

THE FIRST BULLET PIERCED HIS ABDOMEN. THE SECOND GRAZED HIS LEFT SHOULDER AND WOUNDED TWO BYSTANDERS.

THE GUNMAN IS A 23-YEAR-OLD TURK, MEHMET ALI AGCA— A MURDERER ESCAPED FROM PRISON. YOU WILL RECALL THAT HE HAD ALREADY THREATENED TO KILL THE POPE DURING HIS VISIT TO TURKEY.

EITHER ISLAMIC RADICALS OR THE SOVIET SECRET SERVICE ARE BEHIND THIS!

16

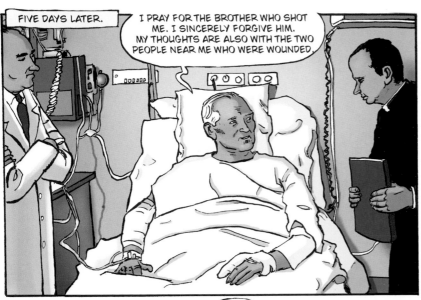

FIVE DAYS LATER.

I PRAY FOR THE BROTHER WHO SHOT ME. I SINCERELY FORGIVE HIM. MY THOUGHTS ARE ALSO WITH THE TWO PEOPLE NEAR ME WHO WERE WOUNDED.

DESPITE HIS STAY IN THE CLINIC, THE HOLY FATHER DOES NOT STOP WORKING.

DID YOU SEE THE GET-WELL TELEGRAM THAT BREZHNEV SENT ME? AND WHILE I'VE BEEN HERE, ITALY HAS VOTED TO EXTEND ACCESS TO ABORTION.

AGAINST THE ADVICE OF HIS DOCTORS, HE IS BACK AT THE VATICAN ON MAY 28, 1981.

CARDINAL WYSZYŃSKI, MY VERY DEAR FRIEND, HAS PASSED AWAY. WITHOUT HIM, I COULD NEVER HAVE BECOME POPE.

IN VIEW OF EVENTS, OUR POOR POLAND NEEDS A SHEPHERD NOW MORE THAN EVER!

ON JULY 7, THE BISHOP OF WARMIA, JÓZEF GLEMP, IS NAMED PRIMATE OF POLAND AND ARCHBISHOP OF GNIEZNO AND WARSAW—A WEIGHTY TASK, GIVEN THE TENSE POLITICAL SITUATION.

THE HOLY FATHER HAS HONORED ME WITH HIS CONFIDENCE. I WILL CARRY ON THE CARDINAL'S WORK.

THE WINTER IS PARTICULARLY "HOT" IN THAT YEAR OF 1981. ON DECEMBER 13, MARTIAL LAW* IS DECLARED IN POLAND.

MANY OF THOSE WHO HAVE CRITICIZED THE GOVERNMENT HAVE BEEN ARRESTED,** INCLUDING LECH WAŁĘSA!

JUST BE GLAD THAT THE RUSSIANS HAVEN'T GOTTEN INVOLVED. POLAND IS NOW CUT OFF FROM THE WORLD. OH, LOOK OUT!

* RULE BY THE MILITARY
** OVER 10,000 PEOPLE IN 48 PRISONS AND INTERNMENT CAMPS

ALL PUBLIC GATHERINGS ARE BANNED. CURFEW IS SET AT 10:00 P.M.!

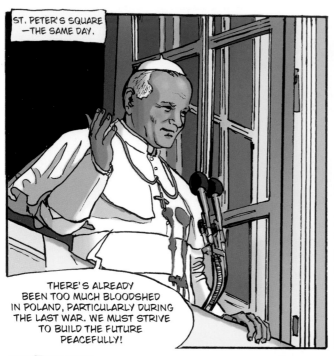

ST. PETER'S SQUARE —THE SAME DAY.

THERE'S ALREADY BEEN TOO MUCH BLOODSHED IN POLAND, PARTICULARLY DURING THE LAST WAR. WE MUST STRIVE TO BUILD THE FUTURE PEACEFULLY!

THE POLISH CHURCH IS UNDER PRESSURE TO STOP ITS OPPOSITION TO COMMUNISM, BUT WITH PERSEVERANCE IT WILL WIN IN THE END.

COURAGE, MY FRIENDS! THE HOLY FATHER PLANS TO VISIT POLAND VERY SOON, AND THE WEST WILL SUPPLY US WITH FOOD SHORTLY. AS TO JARUZELSKI, HE KNOWS VERY WELL THAT HIS REGIME IS DOOMED.

AT THE END OF 1981, THE HOLY FATHER APPOINTS JOSEPH CARDINAL RATZINGER, ARCHBISHOP OF MUNICH-FREISING, PREFECT OF THE CONGREGATION FOR THE DOCTRINE OF THE FAITH.

THE CHURCH IS BLESSED: JOHN PAUL II, THE POLISH PHILOSOPHER, AND CARDINAL RATZINGER, THE GERMAN THEOLOGIAN.

DESPITE THE CRISIS IN POLAND, IN 1982 THE POPE CONTINUES HIS MANY TRAVELS: HE VISITS AFRICA, GREAT BRITAIN, BRAZIL, ARGENTINA, SPAIN, AND PORTUGAL!

1983 BEGINS WITH A VISIT TO CENTRAL AMERICA, THEN, AT LAST, FROM JUNE 16 TO 23, TO POLAND, WHERE LECH WAŁĘSA HAD BEEN FREED.*

THE VISIT OF YOUR HOLINESS TESTIFIES TO THE GRADUAL STABILIZATION OF LIFE IN OUR COUNTRY!

HE VISITS LOURDES FOR THE FEAST OF THE ASSUMPTION.

IT'S A LIE! LOOK, SIR, HOW SAD THE HOLY FATHER LOOKS! HE'S NOT FOOLED BY YOU!

FATIMA: MAY 13 IS THE ANNIVERSARY OF THE ATTACK ON THE POPE IN ROME, BUT ALSO OF THE FIRST APPARITION OF OUR LADY TO THREE SHEPHERD CHILDREN. THE HOLY FATHER GIVES THANKS TO GOD AND MARY FOR HAVING SAVED HIM.

* HE RETURNED HOME UNDER STRICT SURVEILLANCE ON NOVEMBER 12, 1982.

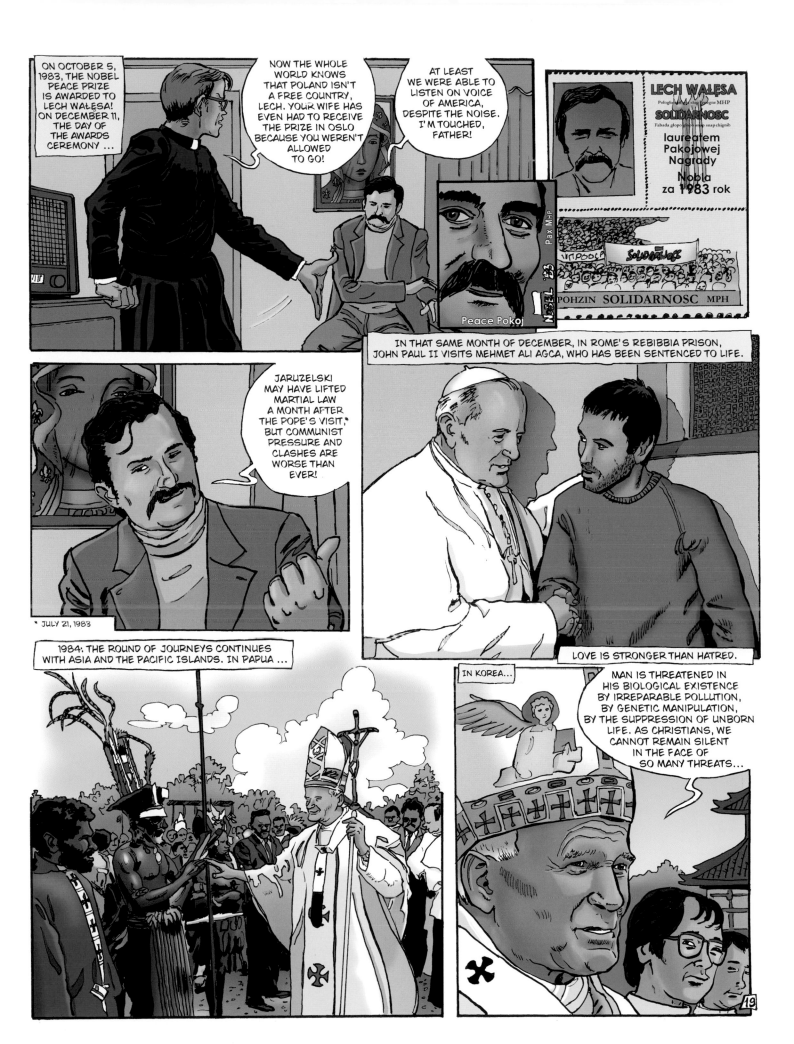

THEN TO GENEVA, SWITZERLAND. HE MAKES A SPEECH TO THE WORLD COUNCIL OF CHURCHES.

THIS COOL RECEPTION WAS TO BE EXPECTED. THE WCC* HAS NEVER INVOLVED ITSELF MUCH WITH PERSECUTED CHRISTIANS IN EASTERN EUROPE.

*AN INSTITUTION MADE UP OF MOST REFORMED AND ORTHODOX CHURCHES.

THEY HAVE BEEN MORE CONCERNED WITH THE PROBLEMS OF POOR, DEVELOPING COUNTRIES.

YES! JOHN PAUL II COULD NOT RESIST THE TEMPTATION TO GO SKIING! ON JULY 18, ON THE SLOPES OF THE ADAMELLO GLACIER OVERLOOKING THE CITY OF TRENT ...

IN SEPTEMBER, FOR THE FIRST TIME IN ITS HISTORY, CANADA IS HOST TO THE SUPREME PONTIFF.

YOUR ENCOUNTER WITH THE GOSPEL NOT ONLY ENRICHED YOU— IT ALSO ENRICHED THE CHURCH!

BACK IN ROME, AFTER ANOTHER TOUR OF THE ANTILLES.

DESPITE THE AMNESTY OF POLITICAL PRISONERS, THE ATMOSPHERE IN POLAND IS STILL TENSE.

ACTS OF VIOLENCE BY THE PRO-SOVIET HARDLINERS ARE MORE AND MORE FREQUENT: THEY WANT TO GET RID OF JARUZELSKI, WHO THEY THINK IS TOO SOFT!

DURING THE NIGHT OF OCTOBER 19.

FATHER JERZY POPIEŁUSZKO, PLEASE FOLLOW US WITH YOUR CHAUFFEUR!

A SIMPLE BREATHALYZER TEST. THIS WON'T TAKE LONG!

THE CHAUFFEUR MANAGES TO ESCAPE. TEN DAYS LATER, THE BODY OF THE PRIEST IS FOUND, BOUND AND TORTURED, IN A BRANCH OF THE VISTULA.**

** A RIVER IN WARSAW

REMEMBER CHRIST WEEPING AT THE DEATH OF HIS FRIEND LAZARUS! LET US NOT US GIVE WAY TO ANGER!

THE WHOLE WORLD IS MOVED BY THE MARTYRDOM OF FATHER POPIEŁUSZKO, WHO BECOMES THE SYMBOL OF THE PEOPLE'S STRUGGLE FOR FREEDOM.

CATHOLIC UNITY, THREATENED BY DIFFERING FACTIONS, IS ALSO OF MAJOR CONCERN TO THE HOLY FATHER. IN MAY 1985,* A TRIP TO THE NETHERLANDS IS PARTICULARLY AGITATED.

DIALOGUE WITH SOME DUTCH CATHOLICS IS IMPOSSIBLE.

IN UTRECHT, CATHOLIC DEMONSTRATORS DIDN'T HESITATE TO THROW EGGS AND SMOKE BOMBS AT THE POPEMOBILE!

NOTHING IS IMPOSSIBLE WITH GOD. HAVE FAITH IN THOSE CROWDS OF YOUNG PEOPLE WHO WERE SO ENTHUSIASTIC IN AMERSFOORT!**

* FROM MAY 11 TO 15   ** NEAR AMSTERDAM

THE FOLLOWING DAYS IN LUXEMBOURG AND BELGIUM ARE MUCH CALMER. JOHN PAUL II CELEBRATES HIS 65TH BIRTHDAY AT THE MARIAN SHRINE OF BEAURAING.***

*** THE VIRGIN APPEARED 33 TIMES TO 5 CHILDREN BETWEEN NOVEMBER 29, 1932, AND JANUARY 3, 1933.

ON THE WAY BACK FROM HIS THIRD TRIP TO AFRICA,**** HE STOPS IN MOROCCO AT THE REQUEST OF KING HASSAN II. BEFORE 80,000 MUSLIMS ...

AMAZING! SEE HOW THEY LISTEN TO THE POPE WITH SUCH RESPECT! THE DUTCH WHO DISAGREE WITH HIM COULD TAKE A PAGE OUT OF THEIR BOOK!

**** FROM AUGUST 8 TO 19

JANUARY 31, 1986: THE START OF A 10-DAY TRIP TO INDIA. JOHN PAUL II MEETS MOTHER TERESA IN CALCUTTA.

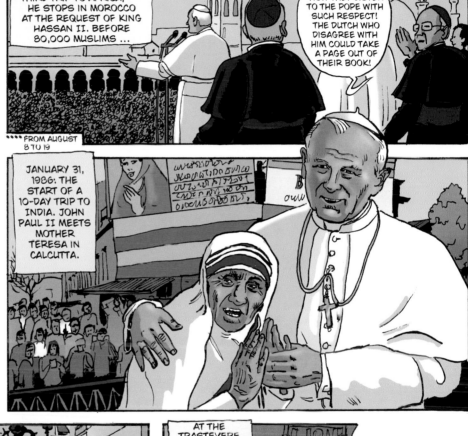

JOHN PAUL II IS DETERMINED TO RENEW DIALOGUE WITH JUDAISM, SUSPENDED FOR 19 CENTURIES. ON APRIL 19, HE IS RECEIVED BY THE CHIEF RABBI OF ROME, ELIO TOAFF.

THIS MEETING IS THE WILL OF GOD. JEWS AND CATHOLICS ARE BEGINNING A NEW CHAPTER.

AT THE TRASTEVERE SYNAGOGUE.

THE JEWISH PEOPLE ARE NOT GUILTY OF THE DEATH OF CHRIST!

21

OCTOBER 4, 1986, THE FEAST OF SAINT FRANCIS OF ASSISI.

I'M CONFUSED BY THIS NEW DECISION OF THE HOLY FATHER! HE'S PLANNING A GREAT GATHERING ON OCTOBER 27 WITH NON-CATHOLIC AND NON-CHRISTIAN RELIGIOUS LEADERS FROM THE FOUR CORNERS OF THE GLOBE.

HE'S BEEN WORKING ON THIS ALL YEAR WITH CARDINALS ARINZE* AND ETCHEGARAY.** IT'S A WORLD DAY OF PRAYER FOR PEACE.

* SECRETARIAT FOR NON-CHRISTIANS
** COUNCIL FOR JUSTICE AND PEACE

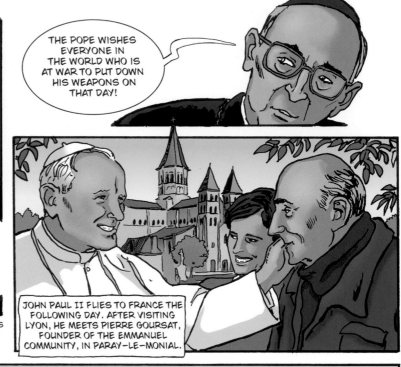

THE POPE WISHES EVERYONE IN THE WORLD WHO IS AT WAR TO PUT DOWN HIS WEAPONS ON THAT DAY!

JOHN PAUL II FLIES TO FRANCE THE FOLLOWING DAY. AFTER VISITING LYON, HE MEETS PIERRE GOURSAT, FOUNDER OF THE EMMANUEL COMMUNITY, IN PARAY-LE-MONIAL.

THEN TO THE ECUMENICAL MONASTERY OF TAIZÉ, FOUNDED BY BROTHER ROGER SCHUTZ IN 1940.

TAIZÉ IS TRULY THAT "LITTLE SPRING-TIME" SO DEAR TO POPE JOHN.*** I SALUTE YOUR LONGING FOR THE RECONCILIATION OF ALL CHRISTIANS!

*** A REFERENCE TO JOHN XXIII'S WORDS TO BROTHER ROGER

AND, ON OCTOBER 27, 1986, THE RELIGIOUS LEADERS OF TWELVE FAITHS—REPRESENTING 3 BILLION BELIEVERS—GATHER IN ASSISI, THE CITY OF SAINT FRANCIS.

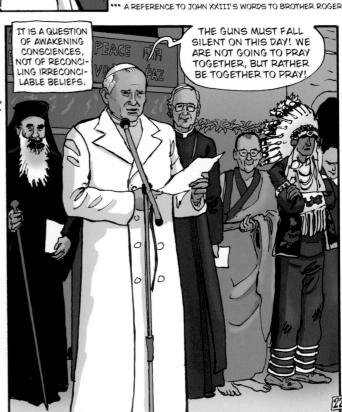

IT IS A QUESTION OF AWAKENING CONSCIENCES, NOT OF RECONCILING IRRECONCILABLE BELIEFS.

THE GUNS MUST FALL SILENT ON THIS DAY! WE ARE NOT GOING TO PRAY TOGETHER, BUT RATHER BE TOGETHER TO PRAY!

22

AT AN IMPORTANT SYNOD* IN OCTOBER, THE HOLY FATHER REAFFIRMS HIS DETERMINATION TO ENCOURAGE THE VOCATION OF THE LAITY IN THE WORLD.

THE CHURCH MUST NOT BE THE PRIVATE PRESERVE OF THE CLERGY. THROUGH THEIR BAPTISM, LAYPEOPLE HAVE THE RIGHT AND THE DUTY TO PLAY THEIR PART!

* A SYNOD ON THE LAITY, GATHERING 232 BISHOPS AND 60 LAY PEOPLE

BEING A CHRISTIAN IS A FULL-TIME JOB!

THE SOVEREIGN PONTIFF IS NOT AFRAID TO REMIND CERTAIN SOUTH AMERICAN GOVERNMENTS OF THEIR DUTIES. PARAGUAY, MAY 1988 ...

LIBERTY, JUSTICE, AND PARTICIPATION ARE ESSENTIAL ELEMENTS IN THE CONSTRUCTION OF AN AUTHENTIC DEMOCRACY.

YES, SANTIAGO, ONE OF THE OLDEST PILGRIM SITES IN CHRISTIANITY! WE'LL GATHER TOGETHER WITH THE HOLY FATHER FOR WORLD YOUTH DAY.

1989: A KEY YEAR FOR WORLD PEACE AND A YEAR OF TRAVELS—TO AFRICA AGAIN, NORTHERN EUROPE, AND IN AUGUST, TO SANTIAGO DE COMPOSTELA.

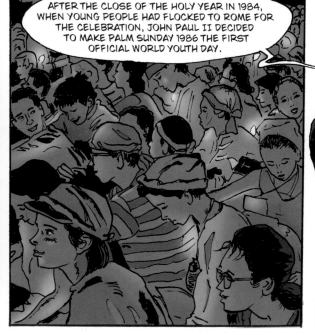

AFTER THE CLOSE OF THE HOLY YEAR IN 1984, WHEN YOUNG PEOPLE HAD FLOCKED TO ROME FOR THE CELEBRATION, JOHN PAUL II DECIDED TO MAKE PALM SUNDAY 1986 THE FIRST OFFICIAL WORLD YOUTH DAY.

YOU KNOW HOW HE LOVES YOU AND COUNTS ON YOU!

SINCE 1987, WHEN THE PILGRIMAGE TOOK PLACE IN BUENOS AIRES, ARGENTINA, WORLD YOUTH DAY HAS BEEN HELD EVERY 2 YEARS IN THE PRESENCE OF THE POPE.

AND SO, ON AUGUST 20, 1989 ...

BE MATURE AND HAPPY MEN AND WOMEN. DO NOT BE AFRAID TO BE SAINTS! THAT IS THE FREEDOM FOR WHICH CHRIST SET US FREE. DEAR YOUNG PEOPLE, LET YOURSELVES BE WON OVER BY HIM!

SINCE 1985, THE NEW LEADER OF THE USSR, MIKHAIL GORBACHEV, IS FACED WITH A CATASTROPHIC ECONOMIC SITUATION.

IN POLAND, ON JANUARY 18, 1989, THE SOLIDARITY UNION IS FINALLY RECOGNIZED. AFTER PARTIALLY FREE ELECTIONS, ON SEPTEMBER 12...

AT LAST, WE HAVE A NON-COMMUNIST PRIME MINISTER!

WE'VE BEEN WAITING FOR THIS FOR 40 YEARS!

PRIME MINISTER TADEUSZ MAZOWIECKI! THE SOLIDARITY ADVISER WHO JUST 8 YEARS AGO WAS DOING TIME IN COMMUNIST JAILS!

Podoski Sverov

THE SAME SOLIDARITY THAT WON SUCH A BRILLIANT VICTORY IN THE ELECTIONS ON JUNE 18!

JARUZELSKI, NOW THE PRESIDENT OF THE REPUBLIC, IS LEARNING TO MIX WATER WITH WINE!

WITH HIS "RED" WINE, OF COURSE! HA HA!

HUNGARY OPENS ITS BORDERS. IN EAST GERMANY, DEMONSTRATIONS ARE ON THE RISE. THE GOVERNMENT RESIGNS. TENS OF THOUSANDS FLEE TOWARD CZECHOSLOVAKIA.

IT SEEMS THAT HONECKER* HAS RESIGNED!

THINGS ARE HAPPENING SO FAST! YOU SEE! WE SHOULD HAVE STAYED PUT. IT'S JUST LIKE OUR PRIEST SAID!

* FIRST SECRETARY OF THE EAST GERMAN COMMUNIST PARTY

25

65

ON NOVEMBER 9, THE FALL OF THE BERLIN WALL.* THERE IS HOPE!

FREE AT LAST!

VICTORY

DICTATORSHIP HAS ENDED!

VRF

FREEDOM

* BUILT BY THE COMMUNISTS ON APRIL 9, 1961, TO KEEP EAST GERMANS OUT OF WEST BERLIN, FROM WHERE THEY COULD ESCAPE TO FREEDOM IN WEST GERMANY

THE MOST POWERFUL SYMBOL OF THE COLD WAR HAD JUST COLLAPSED.

THE TWO GERMANYS WILL NOW BE REUNIFIED* —YOU CAN COUNT ON IT!

MARX IS DEAD! JESUS LIVES!

* OCTOBER 3, 1991

IT WAS NOT GUNS THAT BROUGHT THE WALL DOWN, BUT THE COURAGE AND FAITH OF PEOPLE.

DECEMBER 1: MIRACLES CONTINUE WITH MIKHAIL GORBACHEV'S VISIT TO THE VATICAN.

ALONG WITH HIS WIFE.

RAISA MAXIMOVNA, I HAVE THE HONOR TO INTRODUCE YOU TO THE GREATEST MORAL AUTHORITY ON EARTH!

AND HE'S A SLAV, LIKE US!

THE YEAR 1990 SEES EASTERN EUROPE GRADUALLY REGAINING ITS FREEDOM. IN CZECHOSLOVAKIA, THE HOLY FATHER IS GREETED BY THE NEW PRESIDENT, HIS FRIEND THE PLAYWRIGHT VÁCLAV HAVEL.

I DARE SAY, AT THIS MOMENT I AM PARTICIPATING IN A MIRACLE: IN A COUNTRY DEVASTATED BY THE IDEOLOGY OF HATRED, THE MESSENGER OF LOVE HAS ARRIVED!

BUT AT THE SAME TIME, IN THE GULF REGION, PEACE IS ONCE AGAIN THREATENED!

26

THE HOLY FATHER REPEATEDLY CALLS ON ALL SIDES TO FIND A PEACEFUL RESOLUTION TO THE CONFLICT—IN VAIN!

* AUGUST 1990 TO OCTOBER 1991

GOVERNMENTS MUST REALIZE THAT WAR IS A VENTURE IN WHICH THERE IS NO TURNING BACK!

THE POLISH PRESS IS BECOMING MORE AND MORE LIKE WESTERN MEDIA!

AS ALWAYS, THE POPE IS ON THE MOVE, TO MEXICO, MALTA, AFRICA, PORTUGAL, AND, FROM JUNE 1 TO JUNE 9, 1991, TO THE FREE POLAND...

THE HOLY FATHER IS BEING RAKED OVER THE COALS BECAUSE HE DARES TO WARN HIS COMPATRIOTS AGAINST THE TRAP OF FREEDOM WITHOUT MORALITY!

Radowaski vodywa

2 MONTHS LATER,* HE RETURNS TO POLAND, FOR THE 4TH WORLD YOUTH DAY.

YOUNG PEOPLE FROM THE COUNTRIES OF EASTERN EUROPE, THIS GATHERING IS A GREAT GIFT OF THE SPIRIT. THE HOUR HAS COME TO BUILD A CIVILIZATION OF LOVE!

* AUGUST 14 TO 15, 1991

JOHN PAUL II ALWAYS SHOWED GREAT COMPASSION FOR THE SICK. HE DECIDES TO MAKE FEBRUARY 11 OF THE FOLLOWING YEAR, THE FEAST OF OUR LADY OF LOURDES, A SPECIAL DAY. BUT, ON JULY 15, 1992, HE FINDS HIMSELF BACK IN THE GEMELLI CLINIC.

THE OPERATION WENT WELL, AND THE TUMOR WE REMOVED IS BENIGN. THE HOLY FATHER WAS EVEN ABLE TO TAKE A FEW STEPS THIS MORNING!

BUT WILD RUMORS SPREAD. A FEW DAYS LATER, AS HE RECUPERATES AT CASTEL GANDOLFO ...

SOME JOURNALISTS AND EVEN PRIESTS IN THE CURIA INSIST THAT THE HOLY FATHER IS VERY ILL.

I EVEN READ THAT HE PLANS TO RESIGN!

AND NO REBUTTALS FROM THE VATICAN— THAT'S ODD, ISN'T IT?

27

ON OCTOBER 9, JOHN PAUL II FLIES OFF TO THE DOMINICAN REPUBLIC TO COMMEMORATE THE 5TH CENTENNIAL OF THE EVANGELIZATION OF THE AMERICAS, BEGUN BY THE VOYAGE OF CHRISTOPHER COLUMBUS IN 1492.

LAND! LAND AHOY!

ON DECEMBER 7, THE HOLY FATHER OFFICIALLY PRESENTS THE *CATECHISM OF THE CATHOLIC CHURCH,* THE FRUIT OF MORE THAN 6 YEARS OF WORK...

CATECHISM OF THE CATHOLIC CHURCH

... DESTINED FOR ALL WHO WISH TO UNDERSTAND WHAT THE CATHOLIC CHURCH BELIEVES.

1993 BEGINS WITH A NEW TOUR OF AFRICA:* BENIN, UGANDA, AND SUDAN, A COUNTRY UNDER THE THUMB OF MUSLIM EXTREMISTS.

LET'S HOPE THAT THE HOLY FATHER WILL FINALLY MAKE THE WORLD REALIZE WHAT'S HAPPENING HERE!

MASSACRES, DEPORTATIONS OF THE CHRISTIAN POPULATION, AND ENSLAVEMENT!

* FROM FEBRUARY 3 TO 10

JOHN PAUL II BRAVELY DECIDES TO TACKLE OTHER FORMS OF TERRORISM. AND SO, DURING A 3-DAY PILGRIMAGE TO SICILY...

THE CULTURE OF THE MAFIA IS A CULTURE OF DEATH AND THE PROFOUND ENEMY OF THE GOSPEL, HUMAN DIGNITY, AND CIVIC HARMONY!

WHAT A DECLARATION OF WAR! THERE'LL BE IMMEDIATE REPERCUSSIONS!

AND, SURE ENOUGH, A FEW WEEKS LATER...

ANOTHER BOMBING! NO ONE WILL CLAIM RESPONSIBILITY, BUT WE ALL KNOW WHO'S BEHIND IT!

THAT SAME YEAR, HE VISITS OTHER COUNTRIES LIBERATED FROM COMMUNISM: ALBANIA ** AND THE NEWLY INDEPENDENT BALTIC REPUBLICS OF LATVIA, ESTONIA, AND LITHUANIA.***

THE HILL OF CROSSES. **** THE LITHUANIANS PUT THEM UP IN WITNESS TO THEIR FAITH IN THE FACE OF PERSECUTION.

MY MOTHER'S ANCESTORS WERE LITHUANIANS.

** APRIL 25
*** SEPTEMBER 4 TO 10 **** NEAR THE TOWN OF SIAULIAI

28

ON DECEMBER 30, 1993, THE VATICAN AND ISRAEL SIGN AN AGREEMENT. ARCHBISHOP CORDERO DI MONTEZEMOLO BECOMES THE FIRST APOSTOLIC NUNCIO TO THE HEBREW STATE.

ON APRIL 29, 1994.

THE HOLY FATHER WAS HOSPITALIZED LAST NIGHT. HE HAD A BAD FALL WHILE GETTING OUT OF THE SHOWER.

I HEARD ON THE RADIO THIS MORNING THAT HE FRACTURED HIS HIP AND NEEDS SURGERY!

AFTER A MONTH AT THE GEMELLI CLINIC.

I USED TO BE ATHLETIC, AND NOW LOOK: I HAVE TO GET USED TO A CANE!

GOVERNMENTS FROM AROUND THE WORLD GATHER IN CAIRO FOR THE INTERNATIONAL YEAR OF THE FAMILY. ON MAY 29, 1994, AT THE SUNDAY ANGELUS...

YES, THE FAMILY IS THREATENED. THE POPE HIMSELF HAS TO SUFFER AND BE ATTACKED SO THAT EVERY FAMILY AND THE WHOLE WORLD MAY SEE THAT THERE IS A HIGHER GOSPEL...

... THE GOSPEL OF SUFFERING.

THE HOLY FATHER IS DETERMINED TO KEEP FIGHTING FOR THE DIGNITY OF HUMAN LIFE.

AND HE EVEN OFFERS UP HIS SUFFERINGS FOR IT!

RESPECT FOR LIFE HAS BEEN ONE OF HIS GREAT CONCERNS!! AND NOW HE'S PREPARING THE GREAT JUBILEE FOR THE YEAR 2000, TO USHER IN THE 21ST CENTURY.

29

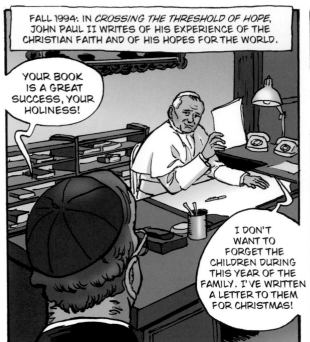

FALL 1994: IN *CROSSING THE THRESHOLD OF HOPE*, JOHN PAUL II WRITES OF HIS EXPERIENCE OF THE CHRISTIAN FAITH AND OF HIS HOPES FOR THE WORLD.

YOUR BOOK IS A GREAT SUCCESS, YOUR HOLINESS!

I DON'T WANT TO FORGET THE CHILDREN DURING THIS YEAR OF THE FAMILY. I'VE WRITTEN A LETTER TO THEM FOR CHRISTMAS!

DID YOU HEAR, CHILDREN? THE HOLY FATHER ASKS YOU TO PRAY FOR HIM AND FOR PEACE!

WE'LL READ A FEW PASSAGES TOMORROW, AND THEN YOU CAN WRITE A NOTE TO THE POPE!

JANUARY 1995: JOHN PAUL II UNDERTAKES A 20,000-MILE TOUR OF ASIA, FIRST TO MANILA IN THE PHILIPPINES TO ATTEND THE 5TH WORLD YOUTH DAY. AT THE PRAYER VIGIL OF JANUARY 14 ...

LOLEK! LOLEK! LOLEK!

KAROL KAROL KAROL KAROL

LOLEK DOESN'T SOUND VERY SERIOUS, BUT JOHN PAUL II IS TOO SERIOUS. HOW ABOUT SOMETHING IN BETWEEN— KAROL, FOR INSTANCE?

YOU'LL SEE: TOMORROW'S MASS WILL BE MAGNIFICENT, UNHEARD OF!

KAROL KAROL

30

Panel 1: INDEED, THE NEXT DAY, MORE THAN 5 MILLION GATHER FOR MASS.

IT'S UNHEARD OF!

Panel 2: THE NEXT DAY.

AMAZING! WHAT A CROWD, WHAT FERVOR!

A DROP IN THE OCEAN COMPARED TO THIS IMMENSE CONTINENT OF ASIA, WHERE CHRIST IS MOSTLY UNKNOWN. AND CHINA IS DEAF TO ALL OFFERS OF DIALOGUE!

DESPITE HIS HIP REPLACEMENT, THE HOLY FATHER REDOUBLES HIS TRAVELS: NEW GUINEA, AUSTRALIA, EASTERN EUROPE, BELGIUM, AFRICA, THE UNITED STATES, AND, ON OCTOBER 5, ANOTHER SPEECH AT UN HEADQUARTERS IN NEW YORK.

THE CHINESE GOVERNMENT SURELY WISHES US TO BREAK DIPLOMATIC RELATIONS WITH TAIWAN.

WE MUST NOT BE AFRAID OF THE FUTURE. WE MUST NOT BE AFRAID OF MAN. IT IS NO ACCIDENT THAT WE ARE HERE!

FROM SEPTEMBER 18 TO 22, ANOTHER VISIT TO FRANCE TO CELEBRATE THE 1,500TH ANNIVERSARY OF THE BAPTISM OF CLOVIS.*

* THE FIRST CHRISTIAN KING OF FRANCE, BAPTIZED CHRISTMAS 496

Panel 3: ON SEPTEMBER 22, REIMS...

THIS GREAT JUBILEE OF THE BAPTISM OF CLOVIS LEADS US TO TAKE STOCK OF THE LONG SPIRITUAL HISTORY OF FRANCE.

Panel 4: DID YOU HEAR? "EVERY TIME OF TRIAL IS AN URGENT CALL TO CONVERSION AND HOLINESS IN ORDER TO FOLLOW THE LORD TO THE END" — BEAUTIFUL, ISN'T IT?

IT WAS A SUCCESS,** DESPITE THE PROTESTS, ALL KINDS OF PRESSURE, AND THE CALLS FOR A BOYCOTT!

** AROUND 250,000 ATTENDED

AND, WHATEVER THE GRUMBLERS SAY, IT'S NOT OVER YET! THE POPE WILL BE BACK NEXT YEAR FOR THE WYD IN PARIS!

AND INDEED, FROM AUGUST 18 TO 24, 1997, PARIS HOSTS THE 6TH WYD. HUNDREDS OF THOUSANDS OF YOUNG PEOPLE FROM 140 COUNTRIES FILL THE STREETS OF THE CAPITAL.

ON AUGUST 22, THE POPE BEATIFIES FRÉDÉRIC OZANAM* IN NOTRE DAME CATHEDRAL.

THIS YOUNG SORBONNE PROFESSOR CREATED THE SAINT VINCENT DE PAUL CONFERENCES** TO AID THE POOR. AS A STUDENT, I MYSELF TOOK PART IN ONE OF THEM.

* 1813-1853
** FOUNDED IN 1833

FRÉDÉRIC OZANAM

ON SATURDAY EVENING, 850,000 YOUTHS ATTEND A BAPTISMAL VIGIL AT LONGCHAMP RACECOURSE ...

... WHERE CATECHUMENS FROM EVERY CONTINENT ARE BAPTIZED.

THE NEXT MORNING AT LONGCHAMPS, ABOUT 1.2 MILLION YOUNG PEOPLE ARRIVE FOR MASS.

DEAR YOUNG PEOPLE, YOUR PATH DOES NOT STOP HERE! TAKE TO THE ROADS OF THE WORLD, THE ROADS OF HUMANITY, ALWAYS UNITED IN THE CHURCH OF CHRIST!

AT THE CEREMONY, THE HOLY FATHER ANNOUNCES THAT SAINT THÉRÈSE OF LISIEUX WILL BE PROCLAIMED A DOCTOR OF THE CHURCH ON OCTOBER 19.***

THÉRÈSE OF LISIEUX IS A SAINT FOR THE YOUNG, AN EMINENT MODEL AND GUIDE ON THE CHRISTIAN PATH FOR OUR TIME HERE ON THE EVE OF THE THIRD MILLENNIUM.

*** WORLD DAY OF MISSIONS; SAINT THÉRÈSE IS ALSO PATRONESS OF MISSIONS.

ON THE AFTERNOON OF AUGUST 22, THE POPE VISITS THE GRAVE OF HIS OLD FRIEND, PROFESSOR JÉRÔME LEJEUNE,**** THE FRENCH GENETICIST AND THE GREAT DEFENDER OF LIFE.

**** 1926-1994, HE DISCOVERED THE CAUSE OF DOWN SYNDROME.

32

72

BACK IN ROME, THE HOLY FATHER LEARNS OF THE DEATH OF MOTHER TERESA AT THE AGE OF 87.*

WE ARE LEFT LIKE ORPHANS WITHOUT HER. I HOPE SHE WILL SOON BE CANONIZED!**

* SEPTEMBER 5
** SHE WAS BEATIFIED ON OCTOBER 19, 2003.

IN OCTOBER, VATICAN REPRESENTATIVE JOAQUÍN NAVARRO-VALLS NEGOTIATES IN HAVANA A FORTHCOMING VISIT TO CUBA WITH FIDEL CASTRO.

TELL ME ABOUT THE POPE!

MR. PRESIDENT, I ENVY YOU!

OH? WHY'S THAT?!

BECAUSE THE POPE PRAYS FOR YOU EVERY DAY. HE PRAYS THAT A MAN OF YOUR EXPERIENCE MAY FIND A WAY TO RETURN TO GOD!

AND FROM JANUARY 21 TO 26, 1998, THE SOVEREIGN PONTIFF BRINGS THE PEOPLE OF CUBA A MESSAGE OF HOPE.

LIBERTAD

LIBERTAD

CASTRO SHOWS EVERY CONSIDERATION FOR THE POPE. FOR A FEW SHORT DAYS, THERE IS A SENSE OF FREEDOM IN THE AIR.

A FEW MONTHS LATER,

THE HOLY FATHER SUFFERS IN SILENCE, NOT JUST FROM HIS ILLNESS, BUT ALSO BECAUSE HE'S STILL UNABLE TO TRAVEL TO MOSCOW, DESPITE PRESIDENT YELTSIN'S INVITATION!

HE'S AWAITING APPROVAL FROM THE RUSSIAN ORTHODOX LEADERS.

THEY ARE STILL DIVIDED ABOUT THE IDEA!

33

JOHN PAUL II ALWAYS ENCOURAGED CHARISMATIC RENEWAL MOVEMENTS. ON MAY 30, THE EVE OF PENTECOST, MORE THAN A HALF MILLION FAITHFUL GATHER.

IT IS AS THOUGH WHAT HAPPENED IN JERUSALEM 2,000 YEARS AGO WERE BEING REPEATED THIS EVENING, IN THIS SQUARE. THE HOLY SPIRIT IS HERE WITH US.

YOUR MOVEMENTS AND ECCLESIAL COMMUNITIES ARE THE RESPONSE, GIVEN BY THE HOLY SPIRIT, TO THE CRITICAL CHALLENGE OF THE END OF THE MILLENNIUM.

OVER THE FOLLOWING DAYS, IN THE OTHER MAJOR BASILICAS OF ROME: SAINT JOHN LATERAN, SAINT MARY MAJOR, SAINT PAUL OUTSIDE THE WALLS ...

A MILLENNIUM THAT WILL END AT THE CLOSE OF THE GREAT JUBILEE OF THE YEAR 2000, WHICH THE POPE INAUGURATED WITH EMOTION ON DECEMBER 25, 1999, BY OPENING THE HOLY DOOR* OF SAINT PETER'S BASILICA.

* A CUSTOM BEGUN BY POPE ALEXANDER VI ON DECEMBER 24, 1499

... A DOOR IS OPENED TO SYMBOLIZE THE PASSAGE FROM SIN TO GRACE THAT EACH CHRISTIAN IS CALLED TO MAKE. JESUS IS THIS DOOR: WE GO TO THE FATHER THROUGH HIM.

IN THIS SAME YEAR, WHICH MARKS THE HOLY FATHER'S 80TH BIRTHDAY, HE PREPARES TO SET OFF FOR THE HOLY LAND.

WE WILL MAKE ONE SPIRITUAL PILGRIMAGE RIGHT HERE IN THE VATICAN, SINCE THE INTERNATIONAL SITUATION PREVENTS US FROM GOING TO UR** IN IRAQ IN THE FOOTSTEPS OF ABRAHAM!

** WHERE ABRAHAM HEARD AND RESPONDED TO THE CALL OF GOD

FROM FEBRUARY 24 TO 26, HE MAKES A VISIT TO EGYPT WITH A STOPOVER AT MOUNT SINAI, WHERE MOSES RECEIVED THE TEN COMMANDMENTS.

FROM MARCH 21 TO 26, THE POPE'S FIRST TRIP TO ISRAEL INCLUDES VISITS TO JERUSALEM, BETHLEHEM, NAZARETH, AND OTHER PLACES IN GALILEE. HE ALSO VISITED THE MOUNT OF THEBEATITUDES AND PRAYED AT THE WAILING WALL.*

A VISIT TO THE HOLOCAUST MEMORIAL, YAD VASHEM.

ONLY AN IDEOLOGY WITHOUT GOD COULD PLAN AND CARRY OUT THE EXTERMINATION OF AN ENTIRE PEOPLE!

* FOUNDATION WALL OF THE FIRST JERUSALEM TEMPLE BUILT BY SOLOMON C. 959 B.C.

THE ISRAELIS ARE IMPRESSED AND MOVED BY THE ATTITUDE AND WORDS OF THE POPE.

I SUDDENLY REALIZED THAT HE'S A CHRISTIAN BROTHER AMONG US. ONLY HE COULD CALL FOR RECONCILIATION SO POWERFULLY!

THE SOLE AIM OF HIS VISIT HERE IS PEACE!

IN THE SAME YEAR OF 2000, ROME HOSTS THE GREAT JUBILEE WYD FROM AUGUST 15 TO 20.

WANT TO GO TO CONFESSION?

THIRTEEN TENTS ARE SET UP FOR CONFESSION: ALMOST 2,000 PRIESTS ARE MOBILIZED FOR WYD. GREAT, ISN'T IT?!

IN 3 DAYS, AT THE CIRCUS MAXIMUS ON THE OUTSKIRTS OF ROME, SOME 140,000 ABSOLUTIONS ARE GIVEN.

IN TOR VERGA-TA,** BEFORE MORE THAN 2 MILLION PEOPLE.

I PRAY TO THE LORD THAT MANY HOLY VOCATIONS TO THE PRIESTHOOD MAY BLOSSOM AMONG YOU. YOU, TOO, BEAR FERVENT WITNESS TO THE PRESENCE OF CHRIST ON OUR ALTARS!

** NEAR ROME

JOHN PAUL II NOW MUST ADAPT HIS SCHEDULE AS HIS HEALTH PERMITS. HE STILL REMAINS VERY ACTIVE, BUT THERE IS GROWING CONCERN.

I WILL NOT ABANDON MY TASK! DID CHRIST DESERT THE CROSS?!

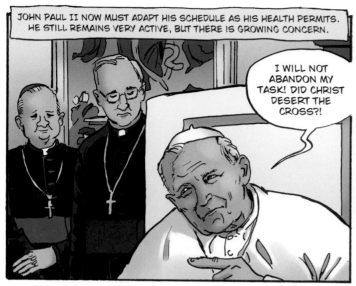

MAY 2001 FINDS THE TIRELESS PILGRIM EN ROUTE TO GREECE, THEN TO SYRIA, AND TO MALTA.

ATHENS, MAY 4: A VISIT ANTICIPATED FOR A MILLENNIUM.

JUST A FEW DAYS AGO, THE POPE WAS CONSIDERED AN UNDESIRABLE HERETIC! AND NOW HE'S PRAYED THE OUR FATHER WITH ARCHBISHOP CHRISTODOULOS OF ATHENS!

THE BISHOPS OF THE HOLY SYNOD* APPLAUDED WHEN, IN THE NAME OF CATHOLICS, HE ASKED THE FORGIVE-NESS OF THEIR ORTHODOX BROTHERS FOR THE TRAGEDIES OF HISTORY!

A STEP TOWARD UNITY.

* THE ASSEMBLY OF BISHOPS

TUESDAY, SEPTEMBER 11, 2001: A DARK DAY IN THE HISTORY OF HUMANITY.

I ENTRUST TO THE MERCY OF THE ALMIGHTY THE DEFENSELESS VICTIMS OF THIS TRAGEDY, FOR WHOM I CELEBRATED MASS THIS MORNING.

THE HOLY FATHER CONTINUES TO TRAVEL THE GLOBE IN 2002—TO AZERBAIJAN AND BULGARIA AT THE END OF SPRING.

HERE I AM, MAKING YOU TRAVEL YET AGAIN!

ON JUNE 16, BEFORE A HALF MILLION OF THE FAITHFUL, HE PROCLAIMS PADRE PIO** OF PIETRELCINA A SAINT.

** FEAST DAY: SEPTEMBER 22

THE POPE'S LONGTIME AD-MIRATION FOR THIS HUMBLE CAPUCHIN WHO BORE THE MARKS OF THE PASSION IS WELL KNOWN.

76

ON OCTOBER 16, JOHN PAUL II ENTERS THE 25TH YEAR OF AN EXCEPTIONAL PONTIFICATE. AS HE HAD HOPED, ON OCTOBER 19, MOTHER TERESA IS BEATIFIED.

HE'S STILL THE ONLY MAN WHO MANAGES TO ATTRACT MILLIONS OF PEOPLE ON EACH OF HIS TRIPS. NOT MANY HEADS OF STATE OR CELEBRITIES CAN MAKE THAT CLAIM!

THEY'RE ALREADY CALLING HIM JOHN PAUL "THE GREAT"!

HE STILL WORKS TIRELESSLY EVERY DAY TO MAKE THE CHURCH OF THE 21ST CENTURY MORE PRAYERFUL, MORE HOLY, AND MORE MISSIONARY!

FROM THE START, I WISHED TO PLACE MY PONTIFICATE UNDER THE SPECIAL PROTECTION OF MARY. I INVITE YOU ALL TO RELIVE THE EXPERIENCE OF THE UPPER ROOM, WHERE THE DISCIPLES REMAINED CONSTANT IN PRAYER WITH MARY, THE MOTHER OF JESUS!

OVER A QUARTER CENTURY, THE HOLY FATHER MADE MORE THAN 98 FOREIGN TRIPS AND GAVE MORE THAN 20,240 SPEECHES. A TIRELESS WORKER, HE WROTE 13 ENCYCLICALS AND NUMEROUS APOSTOLIC EXHORTATIONS AND LETTERS. HE EVEN FOUND THE TIME TO WRITE 2 BOOKS (*CROSSING THE THRESHOLD OF HOPE*, 1994, AND *GIFT AND MYSTERY*, 1996).

AT THE WEEKLY WEDNESDAY GENERAL AUDIENCE, HE RECEIVED MORE THAN 16 MILLION PILGRIMS IN ALL.

HE PROCLAIMED 1,282 BLESSEDS AND CANONIZED 455 NEW SAINTS.

HE WILL REMAIN THE POPE WHO CHANGED THE COURSE OF HISTORY—THE POPE OF WITNESS, WHOSE MESSAGE OF HOPE NEVER CHANGED.

DO NOT BE AFRAID! LIFE AND LOVE WILL HAVE THE LAST WORD!

THE END

IN JULY 2013, THE ROMAN CATHOLIC CHURCH ANNOUNCED ITS INTENTION TO CANONIZE JOHN PAUL II, THAT IS, TO NAME HIM A SAINT. FOR THE CHURCH TO CANONIZE SOMEONE, IT MUST FIRST ATTRIBUTE TWO MIRACLES TO HIS INTERCESSION. THE HEALING OF A FRENCH NUN WHO SUFFERED FROM PARKINSON'S WAS THE FIRST MIRACLE. THIS LED TO HIS BEATIFICATION, ON MAY 1, 2011. TWO YEARS LATER THE CHURCH APPROVED A SECOND MIRACLE—A COSTARICAN WOMAN'S RECOVERY FROM A BRAIN INJURY. AS THIS BOOK GOES TO PRINTING, CATHOLICS AWAIT THE FINAL STEPS NEEDED TO DECLARE THE BELOVED PILGRIM POPE A SAINT.

Printed by Tien Wah Press, Malaysia
Printed on October 2013
Job Number MGN 13016
Printed in Malaysia in compliance with the Consumer Protection Safety Act of 2008.